Revolutionizing America's Schools

Carl D. Glickman

Revolutionizing America's Schools

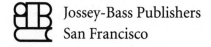

Jossey-Bass Publishers
San Francisco

Substantial discounts on bulk quantities of Jossey-Bass books are available to corporations, professional associations, and other organizations. For details and discount information, contact the special sales department at Jossey-Bass Inc., Publishers (415) 433–1740; Fax (800) 605–2665.

For sales outside the United States, please contact your local Simon & Schuster International Office.

Jossey-Bass Web address: http://www.josseybass.com

 Manufactured in the United States of America on Lyons Falls Turin Book. This paper is acid-free and 100 percent totally chlorine-free.

Library of Congress Cataloging-in-Publication Data

Glickman, Carl D.
    Revolutionizing America's schools / Carl D. Glickman.
       p.   cm.—(The Jossey-Bass education series)
    Includes bibliographical references and index.
    ISBN 0-7879-0944-0 (cloth : acid-free paper)
    1. Education—Aims and objectives—United States.   2. Educational changes—United States.   3. Democracy—United States.   4. School improvement programs—United States. I. Title. II. Series.
LA217.2.G57   1998
370′.973—dc21   97-4826

FIRST EDITION
HB Printing   10 9 8 7 6 5 4 3 2 1

The Jossey-Bass Education Series

—ᴠᴠ— Contents

—⁓— Acknowledgments

This book was a germinating idea, provoked by Bruce Lofquist and others who challenged me to explore deeply the relation of school renewal to democracy. I'd like to thank Robert O'Neil of the University of Virginia, Benjamin Barber of Rutgers University, and Steven Schapiro, Kathleen Kesson, and Ken Bergstrom of Goddard College (Vermont) for allowing me to visit and learn more about their work. I appreciate the competent assistance of the Jossey-Bass staff—Lesley Iura, Christie Hakim, Currie McLaughlin, Pamela Berkman, and Noelle Graney; the rigorous editing done by Bruce Crabtree; and the critical feedback on drafts provided by anonymous reviewers. Thanks to Donna Bell for her able preparation of the manuscript.

A special thanks to my colleagues (faculty, staff, and students) at the College of Education, the League of Professional Schools, and the University of Georgia. The University of Georgia has been a wonderful place for me to tighten the connections with K–12 schools on the most fundamental issues of education and democracy. The leadership of past dean Alphonso Buccino, current dean Russ Yeany and President Charles Knapp has encouraged and supported a decade of such work. I wish to thank all my peers with the Program for School Improvement—Lew Allen, Barbara Lunsford, Frances Hensley, Maude Glanton, Dale Rogers, Ann Seagraves, Teresa Edwards, and Glory Griffin—who have helped to maintain school renewal as a practice of everyday life in so many schools. I have learned much from my graduate students—most recently Corliss Harmer, Diane Carruthers, Kevin Tashlein, Doug Dixon, Lita Barnette, Lori Durham, Vivian Moody, Patricia Fisk—plus so many more over the past twenty years.

Special mention is due also to Ann Lieberman, Linda Darling-Hammond, John Goodlad, Lisa Delpit, John Dayton, Joel Taxel, JoBeth Allen, Bruce Joyce, Seymour Sarason, Paul Schwarz, Pat Wasley, Emily Calhoun, Ted Sizer, Jack Murrah, Joe McDonald, Jeannie Jones, Barbara Cervone, Asa Hilliard, Kathleen Szuminski, Jan

Kettlewell, Richard Hayes, Debbie Meier, George Wood, Margaret Wilder, Bob McCarthy, Ron Mells, Doug Cummings, Jack Shelton, Steve Gordon, and many others who have dropped into my life from time to time to provide another idea or share a perspective.

I am grateful to Pat Willis and Leslie Graitcer of the BellSouth Foundation, Russ Hardin of the Lettie Pate Evans Foundation, Lynn Pattillo of the Pittulloch Foundation, and Paul Nachtigal of the Annenberg Rural Challenge for their generous support of and involvement in our common work. I appreciate family and friends Pete Jensen, Frank and Ann Smallwood, and Judy and Martha Lance, who from summer to summer pleasantly kept inquiring as to when this book might be done. Finally, my love to my spouse, best friend, and teacher extraordinaire, Sara Orton Glickman, for her steady insights about the life of classrooms, students, and teachers.

None of the persons or institutions mentioned here are responsible for what I have written in the following essays, but they all are guilty of having had an important influence on how I think about education and life, and for that I am eternally grateful.

C.D.G.

—⁓— The Author

Carl D. Glickman is University Professor, professor of social foundations of education, and chair of the Program for School Improvement
at the University of Georgia. He received his B.A. (1968) from Colby
College, M.A. (1970) from the Hampton Institute, and his Ed.D.
(1976) from the University of Virginia. He has been a principal of
award-winning schools, author of a leading academic text on school
leadership, recipient of the outstanding teacher award in the College
of Education, chair of several policy task forces to revitalize the public purpose of higher education and public schools, and the recipient
of several national leadership awards. For the past twelve years, he has
been the founder and head of various university–public school collaborations, including the League of Professional Schools. These collaborations focus on school renewal through governance, action
research, and democratic education. These efforts have been cited as
among the most outstanding educational collaborations in the United
States by the National Business–Higher Education Forum, the U.S.
Department of Education, and the Merrow Group of the U.S. Public
Broadcast System. His book *Renewing America's Schools: A Guide for
School-Based Action* has been cited as a standard for all those involved
in site-based reform efforts.

Dedicated to the elders who came before us to open the way—Harold Glickman, Ruth Handler Glickman, Stuart Orton, and Joanna Orton.
And to the children and the next generation of children who can show us how to better the way—Rachel Glickman, Jennifer Glickman Stapper, Volker Stapper, Lea Genevieve Stapper . . .

Revolutionizing America's Schools

—⁓— Introduction: A Vision of Democracy

*I think what you're groping for is that people need more
than to be scolded, more than to feel stupid and guilty. They
need more than a vision of doom. They need a vision of the
world and of themselves that inspires them.*

—Quinn, 1992

These are troubled times for American democracy,
public education, and the future of our next generation of citizens.
Democracy, education, and citizenship are all intertwined, and it is
time for those in public education to accept their unique responsibility to educate our youth in ways consistent with the aims of
democracy.

Once-respected government institutions established to respond to
public needs and protect the public trust are today being scorned. One
of our most comprehensive institutions—the public school system—
is being attacked continuously, with some calling to replace public
schools with privatization, tuition vouchers, and unbridled free choice.
By some strange inverse logic, the term *private*, whether applied to
schools, contractors, or business, is now seen as better than *public*.
Downsizing, deregulation, and other efforts to swell economic efficiency and productivity are now the greater goals of society rather
than the healthy growth and development of our citizens (Landsberg,
1995). Americans today care less about one another and are ever more
reluctant to participate in community and social affairs. Young people have learned from the adults around them to have little interest in

1

creating a better world (Lipman, 1996; "Survey: More Freshmen Feeling Powerless to Change Society," 1996; Putnam, 1995; Elshtain, 1996). What discussion there is of social reform has hardened into dogma centered around political, religious, racial, gender, and ethnic groups. European Americans, African Americans, Asian Americans, Latin Americans, women, men, rationalists, postmodernists, the physically challenged, liberals, conservatives, secularists, fundamentalists, homosexuals, bisexuals, heterosexuals—each, it is claimed, can speak accurately only of their own elations, despairs, and solutions. The rationale is, "If you're not one of us, you can't possibly understand."

While public education is buffeted about between these group forces, the crucial prerequisites of democracy—reasonable discourse and mutual problem solving among citizens—are ignored. Indeed, they are often belittled and scorned by the ideologues. Even as liberal a legal scholar and activist as Alan Dershowitz has remarked that the ideology of groups, no matter where they fall on the political spectrum, has become so dogmatic, intolerant, and oppressive of contrary views that there is "a palpable reluctance . . . to experiment with unorthodox ideas, to make playful comments on serious subjects, to challenge politically correct views and to disagree" (1991, p. 405).

RECLAIMING A BROADER VISION

We need to reclaim a broader vision of education if we are to further the aspirations of American democracy. We need to move beyond the worldviews of those on the far left, who believe the institution of American public education is designed to keep oppressive class, race, and gender structures in place, and those on the far right, who view American educators as aimless, permissive New Age fanatics with no respect for traditional values. Both views are dead wrong. Extreme positions such as these are delusionary and self-serving. They keep educators and citizens focused on the wrong questions. They serve only to make us feel guilty, angry, and retaliatory toward one another. American schools are not monolithic, and they are neither shamefully worse nor infallibly better than they were in the past. They are most often lost in a sea of confusion, distractions, and demands. They do need a moral compass to guide them—but neither the left nor right have a monopoly on morality. What *should* define good education is a respect for the public, democratic good. Only then will public education be fundamental to a better society.

Whether you believe the American glass is half full or half empty, might we set aside polemic differences for a while and agree that it can be fuller? As foreign policy analyst Ronald Steel has written, "A nation prey to drugs, guns, and violence, increasingly stratified by social class, torn by racial tension, and driven by insecurity, will be a weak player on the world stage. It may also be a threatened democracy—its people disillusioned . . . and sympathetic to vote-seeking messiahs inundating the air waves with promises of deliverance from conventional politics. It is not easy to see what lessons in democracy the United States can offer the world when Americans themselves increasingly seem to believe that democracy is not working in this country" (1995, pp. 86–87).

The truth is that America has never really been a fully functioning democracy, and there are now signs of further public retreat from the very concept of democracy. The reason for this is that we have not understood that for democracy to work, it must be viewed as a way of *learning* as much as a way of *governing*. The disconnection of democracy from how we educate our young has led to a lack among our citizenry of the competence, skills, and understanding necessary to live, learn, and work in and for a democratic society.

CHARACTERISTICS OF DEMOCRACY

America has never really been a full democracy. Consider the following three characteristics of democracies (Rolheiser & Glickman, 1995):

- *Equality.* Every member of society has the same power and worth in regard to influence, decision making, justice, and due process.
- *Liberty.* No one is enslaved by others. All are free to form their own ideas and opinions and to act independently. There is no repression or discrimination.
- *Fraternity.* All members of society acknowledge a responsibility to participate with one another in a social contract.

Would anyone claim that these three areas of democracy have been or are currently being fully realized at the national, state, or local level or in the ordinary day-to-day interactions of American citizens?

Our single best hope for attaining a people's democracy lies in understanding democracy as an educational concept that must live in our public schools and local communities. As bell hooks writes, "Our solidarity must be affirmed by shared belief in a spirit of intellectual openness that celebrates diversity, welcomes dissent, and rejoices in collective dedication to truth" (1995, p. 33). The practice of democracy—in learning and in living—must be carried out by those who work together in local schools and within local communities. Cornell West wrote that such work "shuns the limelight—a limelight that solicits status seekers and ingratiates egomaniacs. Instead, it stays on the ground among the toiling everyday people, ushering forth humble freedom fighters—both followers and leaders—who have the audacity to take the nihilistic threat by the neck and turn back its deadly assaults" (1993, p. 31).

This book is about the connection between schools and the American dream of life, liberty, and the pursuit of happiness for all. I discuss democracy as more than a form of government, as an underutilized theory and practice of education—the most powerful way to teach and to learn. Empirical evidence suggests that when democracy is practiced as a way of learning and living in schools, it leads to astonishing success in the intellectual achievement of all students, from preschool through adulthood, and creates citizens who can lead satisfying and valuable lives. My thesis in this book is that until we understand that democracy is the best way to learn to make individual and collective choices—and until we put that understanding into practice in our classrooms, schools, and communities—then the word *democracy* will continue to be merely a rhetorical device that obscures our true lack of belief in and commitment to it.

The following discussions of democracy, education, leadership, and school change and renewal were written for current and future teachers, school leaders, staff members, students, parents, district and school board members, policymakers, and business and community members. It is for all who care deeply about our schools and the future of American society. It is also for those who are at least curious about what it means to be an American. *American* should be more than a suffix to another identity or a reference to a geographic location. It should mean a reflective, value-driven way of life. As Thomas Jefferson wrote, "If a nation expects to be ignorant and free . . . it expects what never was and never will be" (letter to Colonel Charles Yancey, 1816, quoted in Wagoner, 1989). If *American* is to really mean *free,* then an education that is reflective of the definition and value of freedom is essential.

Those familiar with my decade of work as chairman of a public school network of more than one hundred schools (the League of Professional Schools) or my previous writings on school leadership, supervision, and school change (Glickman, 1993; Glickman, Gordon, & Ross-Gordon, 1995) might ask why I should now be writing about such seemingly disparate topics as Thomas Jefferson and the Declaration of Independence, curricula and pedagogy, race and gender, ancestors and ceremonies, governance and school practice, postmodernism, reason and religion, wealth and corporate America, and change and resistance to creating democratic classrooms and schools. The question that directs this book is this: What makes students, teachers, school leaders, and communities successful over the long term, through both quiet and frenzied times? What is the "cause beyond oneself" that I have referred to in the past as the hallmark of successful schools (Glickman, 1981)? I've discovered over the course of my career that this higher cause transcends individual teacher and classroom interest. It brings a collective force to educational programs, to teaching and learning activities, to relationships between students and adults, and to the tasks of planning and assessing progress.

Most schools have little sense of why they exist and what they are trying to accomplish, either as a school; in each classroom, grade level, and department; or beyond the school walls. It has been only in the past few years, after much observation, study, and reflection concerning education and society, that I've become clear about the specific nature of the higher cause that marks exceptional schools. The higher cause is this: to provide an education that is consistent with the dream of a fully functioning democratic society. The nature of learning in schools with this higher cause is substantially different from that in schools that lack this purpose. Most of our schools, communities, power brokers, and policymakers have not understood that connection. Nor have they believed that all students are truly equal citizens who deserve an education that gives them access to the choices, participation, and social and intellectual capital that allows freedom to flourish. At a time of great foment about America and America's schools, it is time to view democracy and education as inseparably linked, both as an ideal and in actual practice.

A thoughtful parent activist, Bruce Lofquist (1994), reviewed a previous book of mine on school improvement, *Renewing America's Schools: A Guide for School-Based Actions* (Glickman, 1993). He congratulated me for writing a practical book about what successful schools do in terms of establishing shared governance, a schoolwide instructional focus, and action research. But then he chided me for not going further. He wrote that "the book would be enhanced [by] . . . a fuller development of the democratic rationale for renewal." He questioned how I could write about "notions of democratic school renewal without a clear view of democracy in society at large" (pp. 42–43).

I've thought about his admonitions and how valid they were. I had not clarified, for myself or others, the foundations upon which school renewal should be built. So for several years I spent time visiting public and private schools, colleges, and universities in the United States and Canada, traveling to foreign countries to discuss and learn more about other conceptions of education and society, and reading and studying with historians, constitutional scholars, and political theorists. Many of the ideas in this book took root during such visits, at professional conferences, and during discussions with school and community groups and students in undergraduate and graduate classes.

Along the way, many people and groups have nudged me to widen my perspective. Many persons physically took me aside and suggested that I needed to read another book or essay, visit another school, or meet with a particular person. I followed up on as many of these suggestions as possible and found myself investigating domains of philosophy, history, cultural studies, constitutional law, and educational practice that were totally new to me. After stepping into so many domains, I found that the view of democracy and education as a way of learning and living, inseparable from each other, has no academic, social, or experiential bounds, only a common focus, purpose, and practice.

OVERVIEW OF THE CONTENTS

To bring coherence to this work, I have organized the essays around the central tenets, practices, and issues of democracy and education. Part One explains the history, philosophy, and political theory of democracy as education. Part Two examines teaching and learning in classrooms, school organization and structure, co-reform of public schools and higher education, school governance, and board, district, and state policies. Part Three looks at the social and economic context of schools and society, including wealth, life, and curricula, and postmodernism, religion, reason, secularism, free thought, and "constitutional hope." Part Four looks at race, gender, class, and culture as differences that help us to understand individuals. Part Five is about changing classrooms and schools, teaching by listening to students, and confronting hierarchy and control. Finally, Part Six is about the real renewal of America's schools, based on the fundamental hope of America's people.

Although this organization of essays makes the most sense to me, you might prefer a different order, depending on your own interests and needs. Teachers, principals, counselors, staff, and other school-based people dealing with the day-to-day world of school life might wish to focus first on the context and practice of classrooms and schools (Parts Two, Four, and Five) and then return to the other parts, which form the basis for those discussions. Those not immediately involved in the classroom might wish to begin with the discussions of the connection between democracy and education found in Parts One and Three before moving to the parts on practice, structures, leadership, and change. Regardless of the order you choose, I urge you to read all the essays and use them to stimulate individual reflection as well as discussion and action among students, staff, faculty, parents, and community members. The essential questions that run through all these essays are

- Why do we have public education in America? What is its purpose?
- How do we make the practice of educating congruent with achieving these aims?

The answers to these questions are too important to be left to any one individual or group. These issues belong to all of us, as we all constitute the public in public education.

It is important to acknowledge that the theme of this book, democracy *as* Education, was derived from John Dewey's book *Democracy and Education,* written in 1916. Dewey brilliantly articulated the relationship between democracy and education. His thoughts about the relationship were derived in part from the work of Jefferson, the *Federalist* papers, and other historical philosophers, documents, and educators. More than anyone else, Dewey symbolically represents the educational reforms of the early and mid twentieth century—the

Progressive era (Cremin, 1964). Many mistakes were made in that era, however, by advocates of reform who zealously equated student-centered learning with democratic education; in extreme cases the result was classrooms and schools that were chaotic, licentious, and permissive. In his later years, Dewey wrote about the overinflated claims of his disciples and the understandable backlash from critics, which lead to false dichotomies in education theory: basic versus thinking skills, content versus process learning, teacher-centered versus student-centered learning. He pleaded that what education reform needed was less disciples and more colleagues.

I have tried to take Dewey's thinking about the relationship between democracy and education to the next logical step, to show that if both are to work well, then democracy has to *become* education—a particular way of learning, living, and deciding (Dewey, 1916; Dewey [1900] 1968; Westbrook, 1991). So although I make relatively few references to Dewey's work, I am truly indebted to him. The vision of democracy as education does not belong only to liberals or conservatives, libertarians or communitarians—it is a fundamental belief about all citizens and their capacity to learn with and from one another. As the legendary rural school teacher "Miss Julia" told her students in the 1940s, "We must adjust to changing times and still hold to unchanging principles" (Minor, 1996, p. 20).

A Note to the Reader

For the sake of readability, I use the term *American,* as in "American democracy" and "American education," in reference specifically to the United States of America throughout this book. I do this for the sake of convention only, not to offend other citizens of the Americas (Canada, Mexico, Central and South America). The ideas and applications of democracy as espoused and practiced in the United States of America is what I write of. I do not assume that such applications apply to other countries. I invite those of other countries to read and form their own judgments as to the relevance of such practice in their own society.

PART ONE

On Democracy

W hat is the relationship between democracy and education, and what does it mean for public schools (preschool through postsecondary), which accept taxpayer dollars, to provide an education by and for the public? In this part I explore these questions from a historical perspective, dwelling on the circumstances and mythologies of the American Revolution and the Declaration of Independence. I try to show how scholarly writings about American democracy contain the elements of a powerful theory of education, including conceptions of the capacity of humans to learn, the role and nature of teaching and learning, and the need for learners to actively participate in diffusing and constructing knowledge.

⟨⟨⟨ Democracy—What Is It?

fter I had finished giving a commencement address at a small college and the ceremonies were completed, some audience members politely waited in line to speak with me. They congratulated me on my talk, telling me that the connections I had drawn between education and democracy were appreciated. During this exchange of pleasantries, I noted a woman with long black hair, wearing a green flowered dress, standing apart and waiting patiently for the line to end. At last, when I was alone, she came over to me, shook my hand, looked me directly in the eye, and said, "I'm an American Indian. Your words about democracy are an insult to my people. Democracy is not a positive, it is a negative that has brought horrors to Native Americans." I was taken aback and could only offer a quick response. I told her that she probably had a very legitimate point and that I would need time to think about her statement. She let me know with a quiet smile that she meant me no harm but that I must be careful about how I speak about democracy. Later I learned that there were others in the graduation audience who, as members of various discriminated-against minority groups, had also felt uncomfortable as I discussed the American Revolution and democracy. I actively sought

11

out these people over the next few months and asked them to explain more fully their objections to democracy and what they would suggest I do to help me more fully comprehend their point of view.

Since then I've followed up with more personal discussions, attended seminars, and read various books on alternative perspectives on democracy and oppression. To put it simply, many Native Americans believe that American democracy is a sham, conceived to justify the annihilation of the native peoples of America by white Europeans. They believe it eradicated cultures that were more egalitarian, participatory, compassionate, and harmonious than American society, as evidenced by the character of various tribal councils and of the Iroquois League (which were much admired by Benjamin Franklin and Thomas Jefferson). Holistic native societies such as these were replaced by an imperial U.S. government that justified cruelty, robbery, and murder by claiming a great democratic destiny.

Similar perspectives are held by many African Americans and Hispanic Americans, who see American democracy as the rhetorical justification for slavery, racial discrimination, and exclusion. Feminists add that American democracy always has been a male-centered, chauvinistic, grand-systems theory that denies women full rights to active citizenship, voice, and participation. Similar arguments have been made to me by members of other ethnic, racial, and religious groups.

Frederick Douglas, in an address on July 4, 1852, spoke forcefully about the contrast between American ideals and actions: "[Independence day] is a sham; your boasted liberty an unholy license; your national greatness, swelling vanity . . . a thin veil to cover up crimes which would disgrace a nation of savages" (quoted in Zinn, 1980, p. 178). Malcolm X echoed the same sentiments: "Democracy is hypocrisy. If democracy means freedom, why aren't our people free? If democracy means justice, why don't we have justice? If democracy means equality, why don't we have equality?" (quoted in Watson & Barber, 1988, p. 91).

Having grown up as a member of a traditionally persecuted group (but not having had much personal experience with being oppressed) and having been active in educational and civil rights movements to give full access to all members of American society, I understand that some people deeply resent it when the American model of democracy is held up as a lofty goal, whether for education, individuals, groups, or entire societies. But still, I cannot understand how any individual or group could take exception to the basic concept of democracy. Protestations against American democracy seem to indicate the recurrent failure of American society to achieve democratic goals rather than fundamental flaws in democratic principles. I think this misunderstanding is where the emotions and provocations occur, and this is why I've learned to be clearer about separating the practices of the American government with the aspirations of Americans toward democracy as a way of life.

I began asking the following questions to individuals who had negative feelings about the word *democracy:* "Do you believe that all citizens should be equal; that all should be entitled to life, liberty, and the pursuit of happiness; that the word *we* should include all members of a community as equal participants in determining how to protect freedom and justice for all?" The response was always, "Of course I believe in those ideals. What I don't believe is that people in power in the United States practice those beliefs." In other words, people who have been oppressed do share in the democratic ideal that people should not be oppressed. So the objection to American democracy is not over the ideals of democracy; the objection is that America is not a good example of a democracy—it is a country that does not practice its espoused beliefs. I found no one, privileged or not, who wanted to change, revise, or abandon democratic ideals. Instead, I found a general frustration in and with government, businesses, local communities, and schools regarding how they practice those ideals (or fail to practice them). And this—how democracy is practiced—is where the hope of education as democracy resides.

THE SHORTCOMINGS AND PROMISE OF AMERICAN DEMOCRACY

The reason why criticisms of American democracy have been and continue to be so harsh is that its ideals are so noble, and thus its shortcomings are so glaring. Yet, this very incongruence between ideals and practice has mobilized action toward achieving a more just society. Those who boldly confront hypocrisy by holding up the espoused beliefs of U.S. democracy create pressure to move America in a more egalitarian direction. The abolition of slavery, the women's suffrage movement, the dismantling of the Jim Crow laws, the integration of schools, equal rights, the return of properties to Native Americans, and the support of religions to flourish—all came about as an appeal to the existing ideals of democracy, not an abdication of them (Zinn,

1980). So, where we sit today, and how I answer those of us who have viewed democracy as a cloak for domination and oppression, is that

- We need to reaffirm that democracy is a way of educating people and of leading a principled life that needs to be taken seriously in our day-to-day practices.
- We need to acknowledge that America was never a full democracy in the past and still is not today.
- We need to recognize that we can gain greater justice and equality by keeping democratic ideals before us and providing every citizen the knowledge, skills, and authority needed to be involved with others in deciding how to realize those ideals.

~~~ Democracy and Education

F amous Americans, like Thomas Jefferson, have espoused democracy as a way of creating an educative society, one that "diffuse[s] knowledge more generally through the mass of the people" (quoted in Peterson, 1975, p. 193). Jefferson also wrote, "Although I do not, with some enthusiasts, believe that the human condition will ever advance to such a state of perfection as that there shall no longer be pain or vice in the world, yet I believe it susceptible to much improvement and . . . that the diffusion of knowledge among people is to be the instrument by which it is to be effected" (quoted in Randall, 1993, p. 205). Thus Jefferson advocated "a whole scheme of . . . teaching all the children of the state," which was to include "schools of the hundreds, wherein the great mass of the people will receive their instruction, the principal foundation of future order will be laid here" (quoted in Peterson, 1975, p. 193).

The writers of the Declaration of Independence and the U.S. Constitution were influenced by more than Western thinkers in their development of the principles, rights, laws, and government of a self-governing society. It is documented that both Jefferson and Benjamin Franklin admired how Native Americans counseled, cared for, and taught their children: "The principling of their society forbidding all compulsion . . . lead to duty and to enterprise by personal influence and persuasion" (Jefferson, quoted in Peterson, 1975, p. 99).

Jefferson made the link between democracy and education quite clear when he wrote of the need for public education: "Every government degenerates when trusted to the rulers of the people alone. The people themselves, therefore, are its only safe depositories. And to render even them safe their minds must be improved. . . . The influence over government must be shared among all people" (quoted in Peterson, 1975, p. 198).

The Bill of Rights was adopted, according to James Madison, as "a good ground for an appeal to the sense of the community" (quoted in Peck, 1992, p. 63). What was to be that community sensibility? A democratic society was to protect freedom of conscience, freedom of expression, ensure justice, and provide for equal protection under the law (Peck, 1992). All of these protections were to be based on human interpretations of what freedom meant and how rules, laws, and judicial reviews were to operate. Freedom of speech; a free press; the general diffusion of knowledge; public deliberation and debate; checks and balances between the executive, legislative, and judicial branches of government; elected representatives of the people; the inalienable rights of life, liberty, and the pursuit of happiness; and justice and equality for all were not only safeguards of freedom but essentials of human learning. The most significant statement with pedagogical implications (though probably not thought of as such by Jefferson at the time) is "If every individual which composes their mass participates of the ultimate authority, the government will be safe" (quoted in Peterson, 1975, p. 199). The decisions regarding how people are to be governed were to be made by ordinary citizens—not dictators, not kings, and not gods. Madison wrote in *Federalist No. 10* that democracy must be based on factions. Contrary voices and interests must be incorporated to gain multiple perspectives and to provide the fullest information possible before taking action for the common good: "liberty is to faction what air is to fire, an aliment without wishing it. . . . As long as the reason of man continues fallible, and he is at liberty to exercise it, different opinions will be formed" (quoted in Rossiter, 1961, p. 78).

The reasoning goes in somewhat this order. Democracy is established to protect the liberty and freedom of all citizens to rule themselves. To do so, varying opinions and expressions are protected so as to inform human discourse and decisions. To ensure a protected society, all citizens surrender unrestricted individual rights and form a social contract that ensures the common rights of all. These rights are to be decided by the people themselves and enforced by law.

Now, the gap between beliefs and aspirations, and the cumbersomeness of democracy in America, have been great. It is questionable if the founders of American democracy understood the full ramifications of the exposed principles of the Declaration of Independence and the Bill of Rights. As Zinn (1980) argues, such passage was more for purposes of compromise and could be construed as protecting existing wealth rather than realizing noble ideals. The litany of exploitation, violations, denigration, and outright cruelty to those not considered "We, the people" is irrefutable—though perhaps no worse and at times better than the exploitation of people by other nations.

How does one explain that although American democracy was to be a statement against class privilege and wealth, most of the "founding fathers" were landed gentry of aristocratic class?[1] What about their stating that "all men are created equal" but excluding women from the citizenry? How does one understand the concept of justice of a time when Native Americans were being systematically forced off their lands and exterminated? How does one equate equality with a society that allowed despotic slavery? A basic problem of democracies, throughout history and not only in the United States, is the definition of a citizen. It's always easier to couch liberty and equality as rights of all citizens when such rights accrue only to a select group defined as citizens (and thus to deny them to others who are not—officially or unofficially—regarded as citizens).

Another ongoing problem with American democracy, from its inception, has been the creation of legalistic structures and bodies that seem to exclude the direct involvement of citizens and obscure actions for the general welfare in a morass of laws and legislation. Jefferson had envisioned a democracy that would always be in revolution—every twenty years or so—to reorient the government back to the "natural rights" of citizens. At Jefferson's own inauguration as president, he announced the "Revolution of 1800"—to remove from the government accumulated elitism, privilege, distrust of the people, and monarchical drift (Peterson, 1975, p. xxxii). At the end of his life, Jefferson felt that America had lost sight of the revolutionary goals of direct participation by all citizens as equals and turned instead toward accumulating more and more representatives, bureaucracies, and

cumbersome agencies. This explains Jefferson's admiration for the elo-
quence and wisdom of the Native American system of tribal governance, which he observed to be a simple and direct way of
participating in community life. His fear was that America would
become an oligarchy, as some of the founding fathers had explicitly
preferred. As Benjamin Rush so accurately observed upon the ratifi-
cation of the American Constitution, power was given to the people
"only on the days of their elections. After this it is the property of the
rulers" (quoted in Arendt, 1963, p. 236). Hamilton concurred with the
need for a ruling class: "Nothing but a permanent body can check the
imprudence of democracy" (quoted in Zinn, 1980, p. 95).

My discussion of the roots of American democracy, its ambiguity,
its history of boldly advocating for an enlightened, free, and equal
society while often practicing the reverse, is not intended to support
the polemics of the radical left ("America has always been wrong") or
the radical right ("America, love it or leave it"). American society is
not always unjust and conspiratorial, nor is it always right when left
to patriotism, God, and the free market. Instead, American democracy is mostly no better or worse than the contradictions and tensions
and wisdom and care of humans. All of us—short of sainthood—are
caught between love, compassion, and care for one another and the
impulses for control, power, accumulation, and status over others. The
question is, how can the forces of selfishness and altruism come
together to achieve the greater goals of a society? This is where education enters and where the futures of our society, our schools, and
our next generations of citizens are determined. Public education is
not public simply because it is publicly funded (Barber, 1992). Rather,
a society that espouses democratic principles funds its schools to educate and serve the public. Democratic societies educate students so
that as citizens they can promote democracy and be more responsive
to its ideals than were previous generations.

As John Stuart Mill wrote, "the existing generation is master both
of the training and the entire generation . . . to come; it cannot indeed
make them perfectly wise and good, because it is so lamentably defi-
cient in goodness and wisdom. . . . But it is perfectly able to make the
rising generation, as a whole, as good as, and a little better than, itself"
(quoted in Gutmann, 1987). Or, as it was said in an eloquent way by
a colleague of color, "each generation has to make American democracy mean in practice more than the founding fathers ever could have
intended."

What most thinkers, writers, educators, and reformers have failed to grasp is what John Dewey (1916) meant when referring to education as life itself. Only a certain type of education can make democracy the life of a people. Democracy must be incorporated into learning—for oneself, from, and with others. Only then will it become an everyday way of life, a way of self-governance, and a way of "walking the talk."

Note

1. A colleague, legal scholar John Dayton, reminds me that "This is often a problem of 'presentism,' calling into question *all* acts and motivations of persons out of historical context and applying contemporary standards to historical contexts (*i.e.,* was Jesus a sexist because none of the twelve he chose as apostles were females? A racist because all were Jews?)" (personal communication, May 1, 1996).

~~~ Ambiguity and Informed Minds

The one person and document that are most symbolic of American democracy are Thomas Jefferson and the Declaration of Independence. Jefferson and the Declaration have been invoked, time and time again, to justify polemics or adulation (Wills, 1979; O'Brien, 1996; Peterson, 1994; Wilson, 1992). The historic facts are that the Declaration was not a document of great significance at the time of its signing and it was not signed at a single formal setting of delegates as depicted in the well-known painting. America had already been declared an independent country; the Declaration's main purpose was to provide a formal, legal document that would help in securing economic aid from France in the war against England. It was twenty-seven years later that July 4 was chosen as a national holiday (incidentally, the Declaration was not signed on that date). The symbols and ceremonies surrounding the Declaration were invented to mythologize American independence as unique and especially noble. The Declaration took on the mystique of the august, principled launching of the American revolution, and Jefferson was invented and reinvented over the centuries as the great democratic idealist. In fact, the story of Jefferson, the "founding fathers," and the birth of the nation is similar to most other creation stories of various religions, nations, and peoples. Creation stories have some basis in historic truth, but over time the people, events, and ideas in them are purposefully exaggerated to lay a special claim on future generations of followers, members, and citizens.

Wills argues that Jefferson was not an original political theorist influenced by the romantic ideas of Rousseau but was mostly influenced by the Scottish empiricists. His call for equality was not a philosophical statement about the human condition but rather a restating of the quantitative belief held to by scientists of the day that "man" was a species distinct from other species of animals. During his lifetime and for several decades afterward, Jefferson was not regarded as a great public hero. Both as governor of Virginia and later as president of the United States, Jefferson was viewed as an aloof, somewhat naive, and indecisive leader. As governor he was accused of being a coward for his lack of military decisiveness in defending Virginia during the British invasion of Richmond in 1780. This picture of Jefferson—a man who died in great debt due to his poor management habits—is at great odds with later portrayals. Jefferson at times was vilified during his life, but years later he was reinvented as the great champion of democracy.

The complete texts, diaries, and books penned by Jefferson—as opposed to selective quotes from them used by those who wish to support their own particular slant of liberalism, conservatism, and so on—are not internally consistent. For example, Jefferson believed that African slaves were inferior to whites. (He did not feel the same way about Native Americans or Caucasian women.) Yet, this is the same person who penned the words "all men are created equal" and argued courageously for the abolition of slavery (but continued to hold slaves himself).[1] He once wrote a scathing piece that described the Negro race as inferior. However, he finished the same piece with the thought that his view of inferiority might be wrong and that it was up to future generations to uncover the truth. States' rights advocates have used Jefferson to support their position that the best government is that which governs least, yet Jefferson as vice president and president advocated for a strong, active, and centralized federal government. Civil rights advocates quote Jefferson's egalitarian pronouncements to support their position on liberalizing immigration laws, yet Jefferson wrote about his fear of immigrants. He believed that only immigrants of English language and ancestry should be accepted. Religious-freedom advocates quote Jefferson to defend separation of church and state, but they conveniently omit Jefferson's references to Christianity and God and the fact that he wrote an entire book about how the teachings of Jesus of Nazareth provide a guide to civilized life.

Yet, what has always been consistently clear about Jefferson's thought is the belief that the people must constantly work at bringing about a better democracy. The Declaration of Independence is the embodiment of the hope that future citizens will challenge current practices. The instrument for doing so is through participatory education by and for all citizens in an open society.

Jefferson's words about truths in the Declaration of Independence—"We hold these truths to be self-evident: that all men are created equal; that they are endowed by their creator with certain unalienable rights; that among these are life, liberty, and the pursuit of happiness"—could only become true through the obligations of citizens to question and challenge the definitions and practices of equality and rights. The Declaration continues, "That to secure these rights, governments are instituted among men, deriving their just powers from the consent of the governed; that whenever any form of government becomes destructive of these ends, it is the right of the people to alter or abolish it." At the time, Jefferson and the other founders were defining a nation for themselves, not for others.[2]

But what we have in the Declaration are the seeds of democracy as an educational theory. A particular form and type of education must be protected at all cost so that future men and women can judge the clarity and worth of current practices and alter or abolish them to become closer to the ideals of democracy.

In acknowledging that imperfection is the human condition, we create the belief that human beings can be special. We as individuals are not noble, but together we can learn from each other to be more wise and noble. This belief allows for humans to determine progress to be made, atrocities to be atoned for, and hypocrisies to be corrected. Democracy squarely puts the responsibility on the people. It never lets the people (or their representatives) off the hook for what is or is not done. This belief in democracy as the responsibility of the people—not the responsibility of a single person, a benevolent government, or a religious figure—is what pulls the "heartstrings" of America and is why we continue to sentimentalize Jefferson and the Declaration. The contradictions out there are the contradictions within us all. Only an education encompassing free expression, abundant dissemination of knowledge, and participation can dislodge us from our current condition.

Now let me be clear. Our current practice of democracy does not work well. In most ways, democracy as a pedagogy of life does not live in the United States. Democracy is generally thought of as citizens voting every two to four years, complaining about those who are elected, and defending self-interest or group interest. Freedom is viewed as insatiable consumerism. Democracy as the everyday way of people struggling to learn and live together toward a grand vision of justice, care, freedom, and equality is usually dismissed as rhetorical and idealistic nonsense. Americans love to espouse the rhetoric of the Declaration as defining a just and equal America and then calmly return to the everyday business of living undemocratic lives in undemocratic neighborhoods. Yet, the grand idea of democracy and education as a single concept allows for the scientific possibility and the political faith that we can live, work, and decide how to be more of what we rhetorically espouse.

Public schools and universities are the only institutionalized lever of education as democracy (Barber, 1992, 1993; Mathews, 1996). As the only publicly funded educative institution for all residents, they have a greater responsibility to practice what they preach—in pedagogy, in operations, and in governance. With a slight substitution of words, we have the central mission of public education: All students are created equal. They are endowed by their creator with an inalienable right to an education that will accord them life, liberty, and the pursuit of happiness. Whenever any public school becomes destructive of these ends, it is the right of the people to alter or abolish it.

Education as democracy is not simply a flight of fancy. As I hope to demonstrate, it is how we all learn best—intellectually, socially, academically, aesthetically, economically, and politically.

Notes

1. The incongruity between Jefferson's owning slaves and his espousing freedom and equality was confusing to Jefferson himself. Some historians have noted that in those times, to free slaves in the South was dangerous: "unless they could pass as white, [they were] more likely to come to grief in a hostile environment. . . . What is truly remarkable is that Jefferson went against

his own self-interest to denounce slavery" (Wilson, 1992, p. 68). O'Brien (1996), however, writes that Jefferson should not be excused, because he chose to continue buying and selling slaves and to capture those who ran away from his plantation.

2. Before one is quick to accuse the founders of hypocrisy and cruelty, it must be noted that we live with the same paradoxes today. Whether one is conservative, liberal, or moderate; male or female; heterosexual, bisexual, or homosexual; white, black, red, or yellow; rich or poor; each group tends to define a society for themselves and not for others. (For example, America is the wealthiest industrialized nation in the world. Yet it has the most stratified, unequal economic class system. One percent of the nation owns nearly forty percent of all the wealth [Bradsher, 1995]). It is only during those times when resistance, pressure, and survival are tied to inclusive and noble ideals do those in control act.

PART TWO

On Pedagogy

Democracy in educational practice and school policies has a substantial base of support. When a pedagogy of democracy is used in classrooms and schools, students outdistance their peers in learning content, mastering basic skills, and achieving understandings and applications. The essays in this part explain appropriate learning, needed changes in educational structures, necessary collaborations between teacher education programs and public schools, and, finally, congruent governance structures and policies at the district, teachers' union, and state level to support democratic pedagogy.

⟡ Powerful Learning

In the fifth century B.C., the demos, or "citizen body," of Athens, Greece, was obligated to participate in the monthly meetings of the town assembly on Prynx Hill. At dawn, policemen swept through the Agora, the center of town, with a long rope dusted with red powder, herding any remaining citizens up the hill. Anyone arriving at the assembly with red dust on his robe had to pay a lateness fine. Once there, anyone could speak before the assembly. The speaker needed to climb up on a special platform at the uphill end of the assembly to address his fellow citizens.[1]

⟡

As modern democracies have evolved, critical ideas, robust at the beginning, have become lost. The idea of an obligation of every citizen to participate in the decisions of the community, not simply to vote, has been mostly lost. (Coincidentally, I wrote this essay in our family home in Vermont on town-meeting day. One day each year, towns all across the state hold a town meeting in which local residents discuss the financial issues facing their town and decide how to handle them. The schools are closed, and most meetings last from five to eight hours or more. A public microphone is available for every citizen to speak. Unfortunately, Vermont is one of the few examples left of direct, democratic participation. But even here, less than 5 percent of citizens attend, public participation is limited to one day a year, and there are no policemen with red-dusted ropes to round up the tardy!) Participation and citizenship as expressions of a democratic society have historically been tied together—in ancient Greece, the Iroquois League, the Inuit councils, and tribal communities throughout the world (see Watson & Barber, 1988). None of these were or are full democracies. In each, the definition of who is a citizen (and thus who is entitled to participate) has been restricted, and the roles of the people and the formal leaders, and their relationship as equals, has been less than clear. Yet the key notions of citizenship and participation have been vital to any expansion of democracy as a way of life. Ironically, in the United States, the definition of a citizen has been dramatically enlarged over two hundred years, but the responsibility of citizen participation has been drastically diminished. Americans today participate less in their communities (Putnam, 1995), and distrust of others is at an all-time high (only 37 percent show trust, down from 60 percent in 1960; Elshtain, 1996). Among college freshmen in 1996, there is an all-time low level of interest in being informed and involved in political, social, and community affairs ("Survey: More Freshmen Feeling Powerless to Change Society," 1996). In the 1996 election, less than half of the eligible voters in the United States made the effort to vote, the lowest turnout since 1924 (Rosenthal, 1996).

It might come as a surprise that the original definition of *freedom* was distinct from the definition of *liberty* at the inception of the United States (Arendt, 1963, p. 32). Liberty was defined as being emancipated from oppression—not being enslaved by others. Freedom was the participation of all citizens *as equals* in defining the public realm ("free-dom" is defined by free men, not by kings as in a kingdom). Over the centuries, liberty (in terms of individual rights) has increased in importance, while freedom (in terms of equal participation and responsibility for the public realm) has diminished. Most Americans now view democracy mainly in terms of their individual right to go their own way and as a capitalist system of free economic markets.

The issue in schools and universities is how our democracy can be revitalized to support and encourage individual liberty *and* community freedom *as a way of learning.* In this essay I argue that cognitive research, personal learning experiences, and ideological faith already provide convincing proof that democratic pedagogy is the most powerful form of learning. Not only is democratic pedagogy consistent with the purpose of education, it is also pragmatically the most effective way for students to become knowledgeable, wise, and competent. I also attempt to demonstrate that schools and universities should bear the burden of proof for justifying any use of pedagogy that is not democratic. They must show how methods such as authoritarianism, obedience, and passivity can create educated, informed, and wise democratic citizens.

DEFINING DEMOCRATIC LEARNING

What is democratic learning? Democratic learning aims for freedom of expression, pursuit of the truth in the marketplace of ideas, individual and group choices, student activity and participation, associative learning, and the application, demonstration, and contribution of learning to immediate and larger communities. Such efforts are made in the context of justice and equality for all, a consideration of individual liberty and group freedom, and respect for the authority and responsibility of teachers in setting conditions for developmental learning.

Before proceeding further, let me clear up any potential confusion with examples of what democratic pedagogy is and what it isn't. Democratic learning is *not*

- Students deciding for themselves if, what, or how they will learn
- A lack of emphasis on such skills as reading, writing, and arithmetic
- A lack of content studies in areas such as humanities, science, and art
- Students all learning the same material at the same time
- Students sitting and listening passively
- Categorizing and labeling students and placing them in fixed ability groups and tracks

Democratic learning *is*

- Students actively working with problems, ideas, materials, and people as they learn skills and content
- Students having escalating degrees of choices, both as individuals and as groups, within the parameters provided by the teacher
- Students being responsible to their peers, teachers, parents, and school community to ensure that educational time is being used purposefully and productively
- Students sharing their learning with one another, with teachers, and with parents and other community members
- Students deciding how to make their learning a contribution to their community
- Students assuming escalating responsibilities for securing resources (of people and materials outside of the school) and for finding places where they can apply and further their learning
- Students demonstrating what they know and can do in public settings and receiving public feedback
- Students working and learning from one another, individually and in groups, at a pace that challenges all

Let me add a few more qualifiers. There are times, in democratic pedagogy, when it is perfectly appropriate for teachers to lecture to students. There should be no slavish allegiance by teachers to following a certain set of materials, programs, textbooks, activities, or innovations. There should be no litmus test of correct democratic pedagogical practices. The current list of "hot" innovations—classroom meetings, whole-language instruction, cooperative learning, Socratic discussions, project centers, critical thinking, constructivist mathematics, inclusion, technology integration, multi-age grouping, and thematic curricula—all have a powerful place in democratic pedagogy, but such innovations should not exclude a teacher's judgment regarding when lecture, drill, direct instruction, phonics instruction, textbooks, imposed discipline, and so on are appropriate. For example, if teacher and students have held previous discussions about the rights and responsibilities of each, then there are times when it is perfectly acceptable for a teacher to say, "I want you all to sit down, be quiet, and listen to me, *because I'm your teacher!*"

Democratic learning in schools is a set of purposeful activities, always building toward increasing student activity, choice, participation, connection, and contribution. It always aims for students, individually and collectively, to take on greater responsibility for their own learning. It is *not* a pedagogy of opening up the classroom doors and telling students to be free. The teacher has a responsibility to use his or her unique attributes—position, experience, age, and wisdom—to guide students to the fundamental aim of learning to be free. Although at any moment in time a classroom might not look active, busy, or egalitarian, over time the teacher is always responsible for seeking, supporting, and demanding greater participation, voice, choice, and contribution. A wise teacher beginning with students who have prior experience with democratic pedagogy will know that he or she can expect participatory responsibility more readily. An equally wise teacher with students who have little prior experience with democratic pedagogy and have learned to be passive and dependent knows that there is a need to begin by establishing a zone that first meets the comfort level of students for imposed structure and then gradually lessens teacher authority and increases student responsibility.

IMPLEMENTING DEMOCRATIC LEARNING

Educators must ask themselves and their students these questions in forming a learning compact centered on democratic pedagogy:

- What decisions should I as a teacher make to ensure that everyone learns well?
- What decisions should you as students make to ensure that everyone learns well?
- What decisions should we make jointly to ensure that everyone learns well?

There is ample accumulated research on learning practices that increase student achievement, learning satisfaction, and success in later life. These results are consistent across socioeconomic classes and race, ethnic, and gender groups. One study compared the achievement of students who had graduated from thirty high schools that used education and democracy as the central concepts of their curricula and instructional practices to that of students who had graduated from traditional high schools. Of 1,475 matched pairs of students studied through four years of high school and for four years afterward, graduates from democratic schools had higher grades, received more academic and nonacademic honors, had a higher degree of intellectual curiosity, participated more in groups, and demonstrated a more active concern with national and international issues. This study, published in 1942, was called the "eight-year study" (Aiken, 1942). In a 1977 study of twenty-six urban and rural schools, the greater the democratic effort a school made—in process and organization—the greater the achievement of its students (Joyce, Wolf, & Calhoun, 1993, pp. 76–78). In 1995, a study of 820 high schools and eleven thousand students, under the direction of Fred Newmann, found that schools that reorganized their academic programs around "active learning" had significantly higher student gains in all achievement domains (mathematics, reading, social studies, and science) measured by the National Assessment of Educational Progress (Newmann, Marks, & Gamoran, 1995; Lee, Smith, & Croninger, 1995). The same results hold true for recent longitudinal studies of elementary and middle schools (Newmann & Wehlage, 1995). The term that Newmann and his colleagues use to refer to the type of active learning they discuss is *authentic pedagogy,* which consists of students actively constructing knowledge, using disciplined inquiry, and finding applications beyond school for what they have learned.

Equally impressive have been instructional studies around specific active and participatory methods, such as cooperative learning, role-playing, the jurisprudence model, inductive thinking, and concept attainment (see Joyce & Weil, 1996). For example, Shlomo Sharan's work shows that democratic-process teaching generates twice the student learning as passive lecture or recitation teaching (p. 8). The results from individual schools that are part of school networks that embrace democratic pedagogy have been dramatic (for example, Central Park East Secondary School, Thayer High School, Burruss Elementary School, Jasper County High School, Douglas County High School, Salem High School, and other schools from such school-renewal networks as the Accelerated Schools, Success for All Schools, the League of Professional Schools, and the Comer Schools). Similar findings can be found in school districts that provide systemwide support for democratic pedagogy in their schools (such as the Johnson City school district in New York).

Cognitive psychologists who have studied individual achievement in such areas as memory retention, skill attainment, and concept acquisition find that student involvement, participation, and choice are keys to successful learning. Research referred to initially as developmental and more recently as constructivist has been built from the work of such cognitive scholars as Piaget (1974), Vygotsky (1978), Bruner (1960), Leinhardt (1993), and Gardner, Krechevsky, Sternberg, and Okagaki (1994). This work has repeatedly demonstrated that teaching that is tailored to the natural curiosity and physical activity of students and that creates disequilibrium between what they know and new information, and then carefully "scaffolds" with appropriate information, materials, activities, and questions, will increase students' competence and desire to pursue further learning.

PERSONAL EXPERIENCES WITH LEARNING ENVIRONMENTS

Being a university professor, I hear many comments from my adult students regarding their frustrations with what they believe to be useless university pedagogy. The following are a sample of what I have heard. (You might add a few of your own to this nonscientific list!)

- All we do is sit and listen to the professor lecture to us. The class is boring!
- The professor treats us like two-year-olds!
- The professor usually answers his own questions.
- She is always seeing that we give her right answers.
- The assignments are absurd. She gives them to us but doesn't care what we think about them.
- She never listens to us, doesn't give us feedback, doesn't involve us, and treats any interruption to her notes as a bother.
- He is insensitive, plays favorites with a few, and doesn't care about the rest of us.
- The class—if you can call it that—is basically reading a textbook, and a bad one at that! Read the text, do the assignments, and take a test—a total waste.

- The teacher has the students do all his work. He divides us into groups, gives us each a group topic, and has us present it to the class.

- The teacher provides no guidance, doesn't seem particularly interested in the course—and we have to pay for this? Give me a break!

- Students doze off on occasion, and the teacher continues to drone on and on.

According to my own students' experiences, poor pedagogy doesn't engage students and teachers in a common purpose. Instead, learning is controlled by the teacher, who neither seeks nor uses student feedback. It is unidirectional, with the teacher talking to the students and, unwittingly or not, denigrating students' own experiences, curiosity, and potential interests. It is not so much a particular teaching method that is the sole indicator of a poor learning experience. After all, some students can speak of a wonderful course taught by a teacher who used mostly the lecture method, but the lectures were organized, and the teacher monitored students' understanding and interest and challenged students to participate in examining and elaborating upon the presented ideas. Rather, poor teaching is the use of practices that lack intellectual vigor, coherence, and purpose and fail to connect with the learner and maintain his or her interest.

Let us now look at what adult students have said were their most positive learning experiences in elementary and secondary school. These are samples of comments gathered from thousands of adults, who though different from one another in their political persuasion, race, gender, and socioeconomic status, displayed remarkable agreement regarding what constitutes powerful learning and teaching:

- My learning was active. I did something with what I learned—a project, a research study, a display.

- The teacher cared about me, knew me well, and allowed me to take risks. He showed confidence in me.

- I showed my parents and other students what I learned at a school fair.

- We brought people in from the community to help teach us. We went out into the community to see how what we were learning could be used in "real" life.

- The materials were current, the teacher was organized, and she demanded that we think for ourselves.

- He always prodded us with thoughtful questions about quality: How do we check our work? How do we defend it? How do we use it?

- The teacher was great to be with, great to listen to, enthusiastic about her topic, and funny. I laughed a lot.

- I had the opportunity to work alone as well with other students. There was a lot of interaction going on among students and with the teacher.

- I didn't love this teacher, but I sure did respect her. She wouldn't accept any excuses for not doing well. She expected that I was capable of doing great work, and she demanded it of me.

- He involved us, asked us our opinions, and listened to us. He didn't always do what we wanted him to do, but, you know, he treated us as real people—with respect and dignity.

To summarize what I have learned from research and from students' and teachers' comments concerning good versus poor learning environments, teaching practices with the following goals are the most effective:

- Providing students with an intellectual challenge
- Involving students as participants in learning
- Knowing and caring about each student as an individual
- Organizing students' performance and responsibility
- Treating students with justice and equality
- Supporting students as they pursue and find the truth for themselves

LEARNING FROM AN OLD PREMISE

When pedagogy is informed by (1) an awareness of the fundamental purpose of education in a democracy, (2) school and cognitive research on practices that lead to higher achievement, and (3) our own personal experiences in regard to poor and good learning experiences, a powerful congruence is apparent between today's teaching practice and a very old premise. Democracy is an educational theory. Engagement, participation, expression, equality, justice, responsibility, individual rights to liberty and freedom—these things all represent learning done well, not only in school but in all areas of life.

The following all limit the extent to which democratic principles can be fully applied in schools: teachers' responsibility to control students' overall learning experience, students' prior experience with nondemocratic learning, the limited time teachers have for planning with peers and students, the limited number of students a teacher can personally know, and numerous external constraints, including imposed curricula, regulations, and tests. Obviously it is easier (though still not easy) for a teacher to develop more democratic learning in a class of fifteen students than in a class of three hundred. (I write about the issues of curricula, schedules, placement, and internal governance in later essays.) But no matter what constraints they face, teachers, as contracted civil servants working in public schools commissioned to fulfill a democratic purpose, should never disregard their primary responsibilities of helping students gain greater control over their education and preparing them for a life of learning.

Note

1. An account of this practice in Athens, the first Western democracy, can be found in the funeral oration of Pericles. I wish to thank Peter Baiter, a classicist residing in Greece, for providing me with these details.

Cara Tucker

Democratic Learning
Structures of School
Assessment

1. Have Students present a topic that they disagree with!
2. Work as group to collage idea / concept map.
3. ① & x in [oral] of class.

① Map out of cookie dough
② Presentation of State facts.
③ Walk thru map - locate capitals

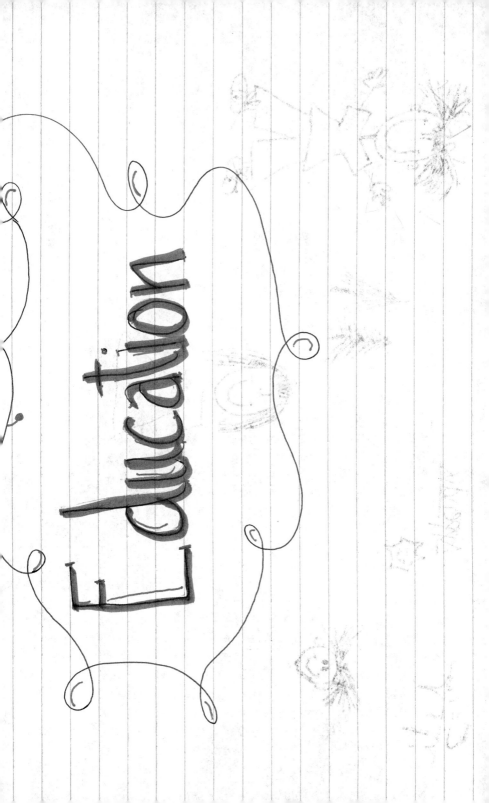

Education

—ᴧᴧ— School Structures for Teaching

Imagine walking into a school where there are no grade levels, no ability grouping of students, no defined classrooms, and no grades. There are few people called teachers in the school, but one sees many adults—interns, parents, grandparents, community members, and businesspeople—with individual students and small groups. There are no textbooks, no mimeographed sheets, no workbooks; instead, there is a collection of computers, telephones, literature, and reference materials. The students range in age from four years to nineteen and are in the school building for only two-thirds of their educational time. The other third is spent outside, working on educational projects in the community or for businesses or social service or government agencies (such as municipal water boards, courts, prisons, elderly homes, nature preserves, city parks, recreation facilities, public transportation authorities, economic and agricultural development agencies, and so on). Would such a democratized learning environment, marked by collaboration between students and adults and emphases on involving the community in learning and on student participation, provide a good education for students? Would students really learn much without attending classrooms containing twenty-five to thirty same-age peers (grouped by ability) and a single adult teacher? Would education be better without a six-and-a-half-hour school day, 185 school days per year, textbooks, chapter quizzes, percentage averages, and grades? The answer is that students who attend schools that are more like the one described above do better academically than do students who attend conventional schools (Newmann, Marks, & Gamoran, 1995; Lee, Smith, & Croninger, 1995; Stevens & Slavin, 1995; White, 1993; Meier, 1995; Wood, 1992).

The beguiling solution for policymakers is to require educators and parents to give up the old image of schools and replace it with a new one. The traditional school, consisting of grade levels, departments, standardized achievement tests, and isolated classrooms, was founded in the early 1900s to emulate the efficiency of the industrial factory; it is as outmoded as the Model T and Morse code. Schools are about the only places left in America that still look more like 1920 than 2000. It is apparent to reformers that schools need to change to keep pace with an accelerating postmodern society. From the business community's perspective, it is greatly irritating that educators haven't already undertaken the massive changes businesses made more than a decade ago to modernize working conditions.

Since research indicates that students learn better in modernized, democratic environments (even on traditional standardized measures of achievement) and since most people know that such change is a necessity to equip students well for the future, why has there been such reluctance to change on the part of many educators as well as parents and community members? And why wouldn't mandates for making them do so work?

Any comprehensive changes made without the understanding and support of at least a core majority of educators and parents will fail, not necessarily because of the changes themselves but because of the way they came about. The majority that opposes them will not be patient enough to allow the time needed to implement changes. Even if change begins and results are promising, the resisters will cast a negative spin on such gains and try to dismantle the changes through greater perseverance. Without the democratic involvement of educators and parents in deciding upon the scale and scope of evolutionary or dramatic change, comfort in tradition always has and always will win out. Activists in schools will resign, be fired, or retreat into their own isolated classrooms and, at best, carry out their work in private.

The hard facts are that most parents and citizens do not believe in or want much alteration in their schools' educational structures. They want grade levels, letter grades, ability grouping, single classrooms, and textbooks. They want today's school to look like the schools they attended. They want teachers to emphasize basic skills and direct instruction. They are skeptical about new ways of assessing learning, group or cooperative learning, critical thinking, and student problem solving (Johnson & Immerwahr, 1994). In other words, parents and citizens see schools as institutions for maintaining the status quo, to prepare students for work and life as they have experienced it.

The status quo is that only a certain number of students are considered of sufficient merit (or family background) to receive the best available education, while the vast majority of students, who are not perceived as so meritorious, receive an education that is substantially lower in quality and that equips them for lesser life pursuits. Few parents (or educators) would state it this way. But traditional schools always have done well for 10 to 15 percent of the American population and been quite ordinary for the rest. To keep schools as they have been is to maintain societal distinctions among those who get the best and those who get the rest. A democratic education is a better education, both for those who have succeeded in the past and for those who have not. But those students and parents used to the best are afraid of new structures that do not ensure a higher-quality education for them alone.

My point is that regardless of how insupportable the case is for keeping schools as they are, without a way for educators, parents, and citizens to understand, discuss, and participate in new possibilities, change efforts for the long term will be for naught.

To complicate matters further, because educators and parents are resistant to democratic schools for fallacious reasons does not mean that all resistance to change is invalid. There is value in some traditional elements of schooling. For example, there is merit in reconsidering whether exchanging pencils for word processors or relying on pocket calculators instead of mental calculation have improved education. There are clear benefits to directly teaching students particular content, insisting upon clear penmanship, and having students memorize certain material. Therefore, there are traditions to be retained at the same time that different configurations of time, space, methods, tools, and technology are incorporated. Let us turn to some of these considerations of structural changes.

SIZE, TIME, AND FLEXIBILITY

A prerequisite for any school wishing to fulfill democratic pedagogical intentions is to create organizational structures that allow for stable, familiar, and purposeful learning communities among teachers and students. The "modern" American concept of promoting smallness and familiarity in education and in business is the same as Jefferson's advocacy more than two hundred years ago of "academical villages" where small numbers of students and faculty would meet, discuss, and dine together. As twentieth-century reformers such as Ted Sizer, Deborah Meier, Linda Darling-Hammond, Ann Lieberman, Pat Wasley, and others have argued, in good schools students do not get lost; teachers are familiar with their students' everyday lives (in and out of school) and closely monitor their progress (while they are in the school and after they leave it), students know one another, teachers know one another, and faculty know the histories, families, and extended families of their students (Wasley, Hampel, & Clark, 1997). Such a familiarity is virtually impossible in large schools where students pass from teacher to teacher for isolated blocks of time and are passed on to a new group of teachers each year. Ted Sizer (1984, 1992, 1996) points out that secondary or middle schools organized around a traditional six- or seven-period daily schedule, where each teacher has 100 to 150 different students each semester, are by definition incapable of being close communities. Teachers in these traditional organizations have to make daily compromises concerning the amount of attention they give to each student in planning his or her work. In such schools, only the brightest, most social students or the most troubled, most antisocial students are known well. The rest basically fend for themselves, and each teacher tries to select a few for extra attention.

Therefore, a necessary precondition for a democratic school is, in the current jargon, to "downsize," to give educational responsibility to smaller units of students and faculty. Schools should be small enough for their faculty to sit together around the same table and make plans for and with their students. By talking directly with one another, they can determine teaching schedules and materials; set proper scope and sequence of curricula; plan student projects, student contracts, and student demonstrations; and arrange collaborations with parents and the outer community. This can be done in several ways—by breaking large schools into smaller schools within the same physical site, by not allowing already small schools to grow beyond a maximum size of two to four hundred students, or by allowing faculty to create their own schools (see Fine, 1994; Meier, 1995). Small schools at the same physical site can share resources with one another to provide such services as elective courses, dining rooms, transportation, and specialized student services. However, each school retains its autonomy in planning, decision making, hiring, purchasing, and budgeting. Students are placed in each school according to parental choice of program, faculty, and facility (within the bounds of district-set guidelines ensuring student heterogeneity). Students remain in the same school, with the same group of adults, through several years (preschool, elementary, middle, secondary, or some other combination). Accountability for student performance and for meeting parents' expectations clearly resides with the faculty, staff, and administration.

With smallness can come control that goes beyond schedules, materials, hiring, and staffing to arrangements for team teaching, an interdisciplinary curriculum, and developing standards and reports of student performance. When standards of learning are developed by small, autonomous schools, then decisions about content, methods of instruction, and schedules can be adjusted to conform to expected student learning (rather than the traditional way, where content and methods are determined by preset schedules, by periods per day and minutes per subject). For example, if a group of students is involved in telecommunications correspondence with another group of students in a foreign country, the faculty can determine the day before how to adjust the schedule so that students can complete the activity. Also, with smallness comes autonomy for faculty to schedule common time for their own discussions and discussions with students, parents, and other community members about how to further democratic learning.

The reason that smallness and autonomy are prerequisites but not necessarily sure signs of democratization is that smallness and autonomy don't automatically mean change and improved education. Such a school can simply continue the features of isolation and fragmentation of effort found in most large schools. With smallness, flexibility, and community responsibility, however, people have in place an environment conducive to change. Since there are few external forces blocking change, there are few excuses not to change. If people don't change, then, it is because they choose not to. (It is interesting how these prerequisites to democratization in schools are in many ways similar to premodern agrarian towns, where people saw one another on a frequent basis, and town issues and decisions were discussed face to face.)

The two most evident conventions of the modern public school are in classroom size and student-teacher ratios. Virtually every classroom, at every level (excepting special classes, such as for gifted students or for students with behavioral disorders), consists of eighteen to thirty-five students and one teacher in an approximately nine-hundred-square-foot, four-sided, closed classroom. Yet, in everyday life—outside of school—no child (or adult) learns in such an arrangement. Most learn in a multitude of numbers and settings: privately, in individual meetings; in telephone conversations with others; in small groups of four to six; in conferences with seven to fifteen; in large assemblies of twenty-five to two thousand or more. Yet, most schools operate as if there is only one method of organizing for learning and one ideal teacher-student ratio. This tradition comes from the "scientific management" theory of the early 1900s, which explains that, to best supervise a factory, one worker (that is, one teacher) can most efficiently shape only a certain number of products (students) for a set amount of time, before pushing the product on to the next worker.

Small schools with autonomy and responsibility for student learning can set teacher-student ratios based on performance standards, curricula, instructional activities, and students' individual needs. The positions of teacher, counselor, specialist, or administrator can be reallocated to serve students better; perhaps more part-time personnel, flex time, or job sharing will better meet students' needs; or maybe interns and apprentices, paraprofessionals, volunteers, special consultants, or outside educational agencies (such as 4H Clubs, Boy and Girl Scouts, recreational agencies, and computer laboratories) might be employed to meet a school's educational goals. A school's physical space can be rearranged to accommodate large group assemblies, small tutorials, advising sessions, and other flexible, temporary services. Flexible management of both space and staffing allows students to experience both group learning and more specialized, personalized educational attention in ways that are impossible in traditional schools tied to set walls, set faculty and administrative positions, and set teacher-student ratios. Furthermore, small, autonomous schools can more readily provide education that goes beyond the physical building, flowing back and forth to and from the larger community. Small schools can have educational programs that go far beyond the traditional one-day "field trip."

Curricula and Standards

What knowledge, skills, and understanding are of greatest worth to public school students? Decisions regarding the scope, sequence, and objectives of curricula and the assessment of student learning have typically been made by those farthest away from the students and local schools. Such decisions are not usually made by or among local educators, parents, students, or local community members. Instead, curricula, promotion, and graduation requirements are made by state boards of education and by the requirements of colleges and universities. Local school boards and districts most often play the role of interpreting such requirements and adding their own uniform regulations regarding schedules, subjects, standardized tests, and textbooks.

A recent phenomenon, federal involvement in curriculum development, has arisen from the national standards movement, created during the Bush administration as "Goals 2000" and now called "Educate America 2000." Under this federally supported program, all school districts and states are invited to use national standards and assessments for specific subject areas and grade levels.

There are attractive arguments for federal and state control over curricula—to ensure a set threshold of academic outcomes for all students in America—but the underlying assumption is that local schools lack either the inclination or the capacity to develop and hold themselves to rigorous curricular goals and assessments. In other words, federal and state controls over local curricula is clearly a statement of skepticism about participatory democracy. It says that education can only work if elected representatives are wise enough to know what local citizens and educators need to do. "The people" are not trusted to inform and decide for themselves.

Developing curricula and standards "away" from local schools and communities rules out the very flexibility that state and federal policymakers claim to support in their schizophrenic exhortations of "empowerment." Most school people know clearly that if they have little control over curricula and examinations of students, then even with authority over budgeting and staff, they have little power to dramatically modernize and change their school. For example, if students are to be examined on set objectives in American history or geometry by the end of the ninth grade on state or national exams and such exams are used for student promotion or public reports of school progress, then schools will keep their schedule, placements, and teaching to accommodate that ninth-grade level. And in the ninth grade there will be a course with daily allocations of time and separate content, materials, and teaching geared to those test items. Outside control over curricula disempowers schools and rules out considerations of what topics should be taught at what level, how they should be related to other topics, and to what degree of depth they should be taught. State and national policymakers, businesspeople, and university experts speak out of both sides of their mouths. They exhort schools to "break the mold," but then, unwittingly or not, they support state and federal curricula and assessment requirements that reinforce the very structures of subjects, grade levels, and coverage that constitute "the mold."

Instead, if democracy "of the people" were taken earnestly, we would let individual schools decide within broad district, state, and national criteria. States and federal education agencies would provide batteries of different curricular configurations, curriculum goals, and assessment standards (disciplinary and interdisciplinary, by grade level and across grade levels), from which schools could select as they liked, or schools could substitute their own plans that meet or go beyond the same standards. Thus, schools in rural areas could give much more attention to curricula and assessment instruments that apply to rural life, and urban schools could integrate the vast resources of museums, libraries, and public transportation into a living curriculum.

An adapted version of John Goodlad's suggested curriculum (1984) would allow schools to change their curricula while adhering to a distribution of general and varied learnings, to include literature and language, mathematics, science and technology, social studies, the arts, career awareness and public service, and individual student-guided choices. Such broad categories would allow teachers and students to dig more deeply into important learnings and applications, both within a discipline and across disciplines, as decided by the local school. Such autonomy over curricula and assessment would allow schools to decide on whether to stay with current conceptions of core curricula by subject areas or to create new configurations of disciplines and subjects. It is perhaps time to acknowledge that a "discipline" is a human conception that becomes rigidly defined over time. Adults in their normal work and leisure rarely make a decision rooted in a single discipline. When was the last time you made a decision based solely on English literature, algebra, or biology? Instead, life decisions are made based on knowledge drawn from a range of disciplines and using generic problem-solving skills. If schools had the autonomy and flexibility to consider and develop curricula based on new conceptions of disciplines, we would have students who would actually view and relate to the world in ways that go *beyond* the understanding of older generations.

Assessment

Recently, much has been written about assessment of student learning. Most parents and students want to know how well students are doing and how they compare with others. Letter grades, quartiles, and percentages appear to be concrete indicators to parents and students of progress and achievement. But the test makers themselves don't believe in the ability of exams and scores to predict future student success as much as the public does. Consider your own grades, test scores, and other ratings when you were in school. How well did such scores predict what you now know and can do? In most cases, such scores have little correlation with achievements in adult life.

Great headway has been made among local teachers and state and federal agencies in changing assessment practices to be more authentic and performance-based. There are entire states that have replaced standardized tests with actual performance examinations. Citizens and parents, however, are not entirely convinced that a portfolio of a student's work or a set of public demonstrations of acquired knowledge and skills rated by a panel of teachers, parents, community members, or other experts is legitimate. The difficulty of acceptance has to do with traditional expectations of public schools. Letter grades, multiple-choice tests, and national scholastic achievement tests are still the rule. (Such tests had their origin in World War I, when psychometricians developed multiple-choice tests to separate military recruits into officer and soldier categories; they later became a screening device for college admissions; Lemann, 1995b, 1995c.) Such standardized tests hold sway, even though rarely does anyone once they leave school and go to work take a multiple-choice test to assess what they know and can do.

Why test students in this manner if as adults we are not tested this way?

It is helpful to remember that there is context-specific demand for certain types of percentages, grades, and examinations at particular educational institutions. The highest degree in America, the Ph.D., is awarded based on a public demonstration of written and oral mastery of a student's own study of a negotiated topic and is evaluated by a committee of faculty. The general public as well as state and federal authorities do not question the credibility of college faculty to examine in this manner. They vest almost unlimited authority in higher education faculty to develop criteria and standards of learning for their students. In public schools, the assumption about faculty is the reverse. The credibility of their expertise is not acknowledged, therefore, authority is not vested in them, and assessments of practice are developed and monitored by outside test makers to keep teachers from "cheating."

There are strong arguments on both sides of the assessment issue, for and against the use of external paper-and-pencil standardized tests and for and against internally developed performance assessments. After World War II, standardized tests were used as a way for all students to have equal access to college based on objective measures rather than on a crony system influenced by parents' wealth, personal connections, or having attended a particular prep school (Lemann, 1995b).

My own position is that faculty, together with parents, students, and local citizens, should develop local criteria for student performance and design and conduct their own evaluations. The issue is not whether to have rigorous standards of learning but, more important, from where those rigorous judgments should be derived. All public schools must have assessment standards—how else would one know that education is fulfilling its democratic imperative? But why not give control over such standards to the schools, which must determine for themselves how best to democratize education, with the understanding between schools and their local school boards that such standards and assessments must be fair and nondiscriminatory. For schools that do not wish to develop their own standards and assessments, then examination by outside test makers should be required.

Placement of Students: Homogeneous or Heterogeneous? Horizontal or Vertical?

There is no single issue more controversial in public schools than how students are placed and grouped in schools and classrooms. Should students be grouped homogeneously, with other students of approximately the same achievement level, or heterogeneously, in mixed achievement groups? Should students stay with others of the same age, in horizontal arrangements, or be with students of different ages, in vertical arrangements? Such placement decisions often polarize parents and teachers. An illustration of such decision points might look like the diagram in Figure 5.1.

Organization I is the most traditional arrangement, with elementary through secondary schools, age-based grade levels, and grouping of students within grade levels or classes by achievement level. Organization II is seen in many elementary schools that have age-based grade levels but place students in classrooms heterogeneously. (This does not prevent teachers from making homogeneous, achievement-based groupings within their own classroom, however.) Organization III is found in many secondary schools beyond the ninth grade, where students are placed in courses (Chemistry I, English III, and so on) without regard to their age or grade designation. Thus in English III one might find a range of fifteen- to eighteen-year-old students and tenth through twelfth graders. Organization IV is found in the most dramatically altered schools, those that reflect how children and adults learn outside of school. These schools have no grade levels and no stable grouping of students by achievement level. Students might stay with the same group of teachers for two years or more. Organization IV resembles the multigenerational world of neighborhoods, families, and businesses (where rarely does anyone interact with only the same age people or only with people of similar intellectual development). It is a radically different conception of school, simply because it looks like the outside world.

But to even suggest, in some communities, that many, if not all, research studies show that schools and classrooms in which students are grouped across achievement levels (heterogeneously) and across grades (multi-age) are better for student learning (see Stevens & Slavin, 1995; Oakes & Guiton, 1995; Brewer, Rees, & Argys, 1995; Slavin, 1995; Gallagher, 1995) engenders the wrath of parents, students, educators, and other citizens. The public overwhelmingly believes, despite the research, that achievement grouping and placing students by grade level is far superior to the more real world of outside school learning. Thus schools that try to change from a traditional organization to multi-age and mixed-ability placements will, most likely, meet vehement resistance by the general public, by vocal and influential teachers of high-achievement

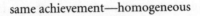

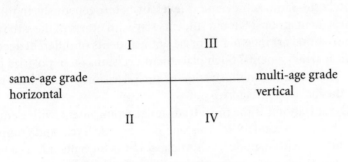

same achievement—homogeneous

I   III

same-age grade ————————————— multi-age grade
horizontal   vertical

II   IV

mixed achievement—heterogeneous

Figure 5.1. School Organization Options.

classes, by previously placed high-achievement students, and by parents of such highly placed students.

Why do such studies create such an uproar? In America, many of us accept that there are fixed categories of superior, smarter children who need to be kept apart from the rest (Hilliard, 1994; Sternberg, 1996; Gardner, 1995). Similarly, we've come to accept that there are fixed categories of "slow" children who should be treated with a "watered down" curriculum and routinized instruction. Thus we accept the terms *gifted, advanced,* and *high achiever,* as if there were such absolute, universal categories. In my own experience, I know of perceived "slow" children who became incredibly intelligent, successful people. But they never would have excelled unless the adults around them had refused to accept the label given to them. Instead these adults treated them as having as much promise as anyone else. It is hard to defend labels and categories that sort and group children in a public institution that is supposed to support and inculcate the principles of equality, justice, and liberty for all. In a democracy, all children (and adults) should be able to learn, to be challenged, and not to have their aspirations limited by someone else's labels, categories, and placements. Every child should have the same opportunities to advance and to surpass his or her peers. Such opportunity is often lost in the traditional school that expects much learning from some and not much from others.

I can remember when I was invited to speak to a gathering of an association of parents of students who attended "gifted and advanced" classes. I remember the hostility directed at me when I mentioned that their children might not be universally superior in intelligence compared to others. I explained that my own children had been identified as gifted from an early age. As a result, they had been placed in some separate classes (some particularly excellent, but some particularly bad, too). But the truth, then and now (with no disrespect to my daughters, Rachel and Jennifer) is that my children were no more "gifted" than hundreds of other children in the same school and district who were not so identified. Instead, they had the advantage of parents who exposed them to museums, ballets, cross-country trips, and political and historical events. They lived in a home full of animals, educational toys, books, and conversations conducted in standard English. They also happened to be the children of two formally educated and potentially influential parents. Our daughters were responsible, thoughtful, and bright students, and of course as their parents we viewed them as special. But this is different from thinking that they or others so defined were really in a class of human intelligence far above others. They were very good students, not gifted and not geniuses. So at the meeting, when I suggested to these other parents of "gifted" and "advanced" students that most of our children were not statistically different from many children not so identified and grouped, many lashed out at me. One parent said that my explanation would lead to "keeping all the students the same, in the same boring classrooms, and dumbing down learning for all." So I tried then, and I will try now, to clarify possible misunderstandings:

1. Those students who clearly are of intellectual or artistic *genius* should receive intensive support and specialized instruction to allow such obvious talent to fully blossom. (It is not hard to notice the eight-year-old who reads *Ulysses* for fun!)

2. Students who are incorrigible and harmful to themselves or others should not remain with other students. (It is not hard to notice students who are violent and can't control themselves.)

3. Students with physical, mental, social, or neurological disabilities should receive various degrees of concentrated time with specialists, as worked out between parents, teachers, and the school.

4. *Every student* should have at least 10 percent of each school day devoted to those educational activities for which he or she has shown special interests, aptitudes, or talent.

The rationale for labeling and having separate high-ability classes, according to what most parents narrate to me, is that, "My child needs to be challenged. She needs activities that will stretch her skills and her imagination. She needs a teacher and an environment that does not aim to the mediocre but aims to the highest standard possible." This sounds right to me. We always wanted the same for our children, but isn't that the desire of nearly all parents for their children? Are challenging, engaging, and stretching curricula the prerogative of only a few? The issue then becomes not how do we separate students but how do we provide such instruction for all?

Heterogenous and multi-age grouping in small, autonomous schools should mean a challenging education for every child. It should mean *more* concentrated individual and small-group treatment, it should mean *more* opportunities for students to be challenged and extended, and it should mean *less reliance on the school* and *more reliance on the community,* inside and outside the school, to meet the special interests of students. An eighth-grade student ready for advanced physics should be studying physics for part of the week at a college, or in a tutorial with a physicist, or through interactive, satellite communication. A gifted musician should receive at least part of his music education with superb musicians in professional settings. Challenging subjects and instruction in special topics should be made available to all students who are willing to sign up and persevere. Flexible grouping with flexible schedules should provide the greatest and most varied opportunities for all. Whether a school decides to accept such a democratic challenge to educate all students well, vertically and heterogeneously, and whether to implement such changes in phases or all at once, must be worked out through a *focused* school forum about what should be a proper education in a democracy that aims for an aristocracy of everyone (see Barber, 1992).

Time for Planning

To plan, consider, and act on structural changes that will augment a pedagogy of democracy is time-consuming. To have the necessary meetings, to consider available research and literature, to visit and receive visits from other schools doing similar work, and to hold open forums with parents, students, businesspeople, and community members takes time. Furthermore, for teachers to plan and attend staff development sessions, to assess and coach one another, to develop assessment standards, to study their collective work, and to present and attend conferences to check for educational developments takes time. And all of this is in addition to the critical ongoing, everyday work of teaching, learning, assessing, and advising students.

Pedagogy for increasing student activity, choice, participation, connections, contributions, and demonstrations will not occur by itself. An abundance of focused, structured, ongoing time for planning is essential. Other educational systems throughout the world acknowledge the need for planning. For example, Japanese teachers spend only half of their paid work time in instructional activities. American public school teachers have less planning time than public teachers in any other highly developed nation (see Henry, 1995). American corporations know this—conferences, planning meetings, and assessment sessions are part of the regular, paid work day. American universities know this—most professors teach less than fifteen hours a week. But since planning is not taken seriously in our public schools, there has been meager pressure for rearrangements of schedules to give faculty more time for it. The typical school might have, at most, biweekly one-hour faculty meetings to disseminate information, one night each semester for parent meetings, and a daily fifty-minute common planning session for teachers of the same grade level or department. To put it simply, to become a democratic school, time must be structured for planning it.

Many teachers and schools have figured out ways to do so on their own—holding voluntary, unpaid retreats; changing the frequency and format of faculty meetings; holding after-school meetings at personal homes; having teachers (and, in some places, parent volunteers) cover for other teachers while they attend meetings; adjusting the school day to be longer for four days so as to achieve an early release day every week; and so on (see Raywid, 1993). Such creative ways are admirable and will remain the primary instrument for planning until schools and communities can control their schedules and not be boxed into six-and-a-half-hour days, one hundred and eighty-five days a year. With such autonomy can come extended contracts for summer work, shorter periodic school days, year-long schools with planning days between quarters, and additional paid staff development and planning days or reduced school days. The typical school calendar, developed in the nineteenth century based on the needs of rural farms, is no longer valid (Schlechty, 1990). Schools should hold themselves to achieving agreed-upon standards, and they should be able to alter their students' schedules, inside and outside of school, to achieve those standards. Students might learn more while spending less time at school if teachers, administrators, and parents had more time to organize learning for the shorter times that students were present. To decentralize to the democratic will of a school is to create flexibility in rethinking all structures, including time. A community without information and without time for citizens to deliberate, study, and act is no democracy at all.

~~ Teacher Education and Public Schools

The National Commission on Teaching and America's Future reports, "We propose an audacious goal. . . . By the year 2006, America will provide all students in the country with what should be their educational birthright: access to competent, caring, and qualified teachers" (1996, p. 5). We need to provide more than two million new teachers in the next decade to replace retiring "baby boom" teachers as well as to fill the additional classrooms and schools that will be made necessary by a student enrollment surge of nearly five million more youngsters (Hussar, 1996). How will efforts to improve the quality and quantity of our current and future educators proceed? It must begin with a common understanding.

Teacher education and public education have the same ultimate purpose. Faculties in both are contracted agents, commissioned to serve the higher purpose of education for democracy. If public schools are to reflect democratic principles and provide students with opportunities to acquire knowledge, understand democracy, and be actively engaged in their own learning and its application beyond the school, then teachers in public schools must possess certain qualities. They must have a clear understanding of the mission of schools, have firsthand experience with being engaged in their own learning, have a broad base of knowledge about the content of what they teach, possess appropriate pedagogical strategies, and have the ability to assess their own work and the needs of their students.

This type of teacher will not exist unless those who prepare teachers—teacher educators—understand the goal of public education and create learning environments that will enable future teachers to graduate from a teacher education program with the aforementioned attributes. Historically, rather than working together toward this common goal, public schools and university faculties have attacked each other and kept their distance. The most recent reform fad, "restructuring," has too often meant one party seeing a need on the part of the other to change, not a joint effort by both parties to assess their present purpose and results and help change each other. For example, many public school educators deplore the practices of teacher education programs at colleges and universities. They criticize the programs for being too easy, boring, and detached from the real world of schools. Tit for tat, university faculty build their professional careers by criticizing public educators as being too convention bound, too focused on control, and too atheoretical. Both groups see the path to improving education in terms of rectifying the failures of the other. Conveniently ignoring the obvious relationship between them (current public educators were prepared by university faculty, and most university faculty in teacher education were formerly public educators), they each take comfort in the lack of responsiveness of the other, with which they absolve themselves of responsibility.

The status quo is that university faculty conduct research and develop curricular and instructional programs for public school educators to use, and, most often, public school educators snicker among themselves about the lack of credibility in what the university faculty are pushing. Even a sincere desire by individual university faculty to collaborate with public schools is often mistrusted as exploitation, part of "writing a book" to gain tenure or promotion.

On the other hand, collaborative and simultaneous reform of public schools and teacher education programs based on a mutual understanding of education as democracy—in principle, premise, and process—reinvigorates what should be a natural symbiotic relationship (Glickman, Lunsford, & Szuminski, 1995; Goodlad, 1990). As a public school improves, it provides better preparation sites for education students and, in turn, additional information about future changes needed in teacher education programs to prepare the next generation of teachers and school leaders. As teacher education programs improve, they provide future teachers with the skills to further change public education. Both for teacher education programs and for public schools, to change in isolation from the other means inadequate information and preparation of future teachers and ultimately an inadequate education of all our students. Let me try to provide some detail. For a substantive co-reform revolution to occur, both institutions need to develop a moral framework for decisions about symbiotic programs. Co-reformers need to

1. Develop a covenant of learning (encompassing mission, vision, purpose, principles, and standards of practice) that defines the core educational values at both the public school and the teacher education institution.
2. Develop a charter for decision making that ensures the equal representation of both parties in developing the covenant and subsequent implementation decisions.
3. Develop a critical study process that includes a data collection process (that is, action research) to assess the effects of programmatic changes on public school students and future teachers.

In other words, if we take seriously the rhetoric of democracy as a way of learning in individual and community life, then co-reform collaborations between teacher educators and public schools need to include democratic principles and decision-making procedures.

CO-REFORM DIMENSIONS

The programmatic links between teacher education programs and public schools can be illustrated using the following program elements:

- Interdisciplinary curricula
- Team teaching
- Portfolio and performance assessments
- Peer coaching
- Extended communities of learners
- Technology integration

- Project-centered learning
- Student choice and involvement
- Cooperative learning

If both institutions are to help each other achieve a common, moral goal, then the truth to the saying "what is good for the goose is good for the gander" becomes apparent. For example, if one party (teacher education program or public school) moves toward greater implementation of integrated and interdisciplinary teaching, so should the other. Likewise, if one party moves toward peer coaching, so should the other. When a decision is made for one institution to move toward greater implementation of a specific strategy based on a close examination of goals and current results, the other institution should support this strategy in its own practices as well.

A common vision for education based on democratic principles would result in similar program components and education practices. It is a contradiction for a teacher education program to exhort authentic assessment, team teaching, and heterogeneous learning for public schools when its own program is based on standardized examination, individually led teacher classrooms, and homogeneous grouping. In the same way, it is a contradiction for a teacher education program to use constructivist, student-oriented, technologically infused learning methods while the public schools it serves use regimented, teacher-centered, textbook-driven learning methods.

When the people in both settings have a common belief in democracy as education, they can check for compatible activities that allow both institutions to gain greater insights and power for educating their respective students. The vast array of teacher education programs and public schools in America are unlinked—both groups take up space in each other's facilities and classrooms but go about educating in their own separate ways.

To begin the co-reform process, awareness and understanding of each other are necessary. For many classroom teachers in public schools, knowledge of what is happening in teacher education is limited to what was taught or current when they were in college. There is little opportunity for teachers within a public school to meet teachers recently out of college to find out what is currently being taught or how field experiences are being implemented. Likewise, many teacher educators have little or no experience with practitioners and with what is currently happening in public schools. In order to understand and prepare teachers, teacher educators need to keep current about issues facing public schools. This can be done by being in schools and talking with teachers, students, administrators, and parents.

Awareness alone is not enough to put the two on a common course, however. Creating opportunities for working with each other, exploring common issues and solving problems together, accepting joint responsibility for programmatic and symbiotic changes, and writing and presenting on what is learned are all essential. Such collaboration requires drastic changes in the way public schools and teacher education programs think of each other and how they respond to the idiosyncratic context of their respective work.

SAME ISSUES, DIFFERENT CONSTRAINTS

I work at a large teacher education institution and have been involved for many years with university and public school reform. With colleagues, I coordinate two networks of public schools, involving more than one hundred schools in more than forty-five school districts. The focus of that work has been to help schools make internal educational improvements consistent with democratic principles and procedures. At the same time, I am involved as a participant or researcher in some of the internal reforms of my own university preparation programs, including new undergraduate programs in elementary, middle, and secondary teacher education and new graduate programs in educational foundations and educational leadership.

In my dual role in public school and higher education reform, I have been struck by the similar difficulties experienced by both in working toward democratic change. It's not that either party is theoretically opposed to it, it's simply that democracy as a learning experience is messy and not a part of the educational culture of either group. It may be part of the governance culture of some universities with major faculty representation on academic matters, but it does not translate into a view of pedagogical work with students or relationships with other public schools. For example, university faculties have the same problems as school faculties in developing clearly articulated programs, creating a meaningful mission and core values, developing a charter for democratic decision making about teaching and learning, and instituting ongoing critical study processes to assess student learning and program effectiveness.

Among university faculty there are the same problems as those found in public schools: miscommunication, conflicting ideologies, apathy, lack of sufficient time and money, and discomfort with change. In both settings, faculties tend to see their work as individual, and allegiances are more toward individual autonomy or departmental efforts (or grade levels) than toward integrated efforts among different individuals, departments, and divisions. In both settings, faculty members are more concerned about their immediate, day-to-day work and less concerned about interdepartmental or interdisciplinary planning. Organizational reward and recognition structures make it difficult for faculty to be involved in broad-based, long-term change. In both institutions, there are faculty who are eager and change-oriented and willing to challenge existing structures. But when they attempt to initiate change, they often must "take it from their own hide," as the saying goes. Such activists, in both settings, tend to become isolated from the rest of the faculty, who are more secure and content with existing practices. In both settings, the vast majority of faculty members are caring, well-intentioned, intelligent, and committed to their work; they have simply learned to operate under the conventional rule, that their job is to exist within the existing framework of autonomy and isolation. The relationship between education and democracy is not apparent to these professionals, and thus there is little reason for them to change (Goodlad, 1990; Holmes Group, 1995; Szuminski, 1993).

Also, various interinstitutional differences can impede change in significant ways. Many university faculty members have difficulty accepting public school educators as their peers. To many in "higher education," public school teachers are "lower education" professionals—of lower status, esteem, and expertise. University faculty see themselves as a learned aristocracy and are therefore not committed to accepting public school educators as equals. Since democracies are based on *equal* rights and power, and since the current status of the two institutions are not seen as equal, it is difficult for the two to collaborate democratically. And even when higher education faculty members are open to the idea of equality, universities can impede equal collaboration in many ways:

- Lack of recognition for such planning (that is, it doesn't count toward tenure or promotion).
- Lack of release time for such planning (that is, other research, writing, teaching, and service obligations receive higher priority).

- Lack of collaboration among colleagues at the university. This makes collaborating with public school faculty all the more difficult.
- Lack of mutually convenient time for planning with public school colleagues, who are less flexible about when meetings can be arranged.

These factors can create an inertia among university faculty in moving beyond the "planning to plan" stage to program purpose, features, and implementation.

For their part, public schools create their own difficulties that stymie co-reform activities. For example, public school teachers and administrators often

- Do not have the academic freedom to make changes in their own schools (that is, they are controlled by the district or state)
- Are not able to respond quickly to school planning and implementation due to the incessant, day-to-day demands of students, parents, unpredictable crises, and community resistance
- Harbor traditional skepticism toward university people concerning whether they will really work with them and learn to understand a public school setting

University faculty members do have greater flexibility in terms of free time, but they feel greater constraints on how to use such time. Public school faculties have less flexibility in scheduling time for planning, and they feel more external pressure to become involved in schoolwide reform efforts (such as site-based management and strategic plans). The ultimate result is that neither group can truly understand the life of the other until they work in the other's setting.

These understandings can be developed as follows:

- Teacher education programs can hire teachers from public schools to be part of the university setting.
- Public school teachers can invite university faculty to teach in their setting for extended periods.
- Educators from the different settings can trade places with each other for short periods of time.

- Teacher education classes can take place in the public schools.
- College and public school educators can shadow each other during parts of each other's normal work day.
- Both parties can jointly sponsor extra educational activities (such as summer school programs, after-school programs, tutorial programs).

Ultimately, the best way for people to understand each other is through the active participation of both on mutually important work.

TRYING HARD TO STAY ABOVE THE FRAY

Before I end this essay I'd like to dwell on some personal experiences with co-reform. As noted, I am a university faculty member, and I have led a rather fortunate university life. Early in my career, after having been a school principal, I achieved some success in accordance with the traditional university criteria of research, grants, publications, teaching reviews, and service evaluations. My rewards have been early promotions, tenure, and decent merit raises. In a setting that traditionally promotes individual efforts, I have been even more autonomous than many others in being able to secure support for new university–public school programs and being able to participate in radically different academic preparation programs (such as the integrated Block Program at Ohio State University, the residential program at Goddard College, and the problem-based Leadership Program and inquiry-based Social Foundation of Education Program at the University of Georgia). As such I am quite aware of the criticism that some university colleagues have toward such co-reform activities as well as some of the charades that faculty members will go through *not* to collaborate with public schools. For example, ever since the Holmes Group (1986) and the Carnegie Forum on Education and the Economy (1986) published their reports on the need for university preparation programs to link with public schools in "professional development schools" (similar to teaching hospitals for the medical profession), almost all teacher education institutes have claimed to have professional development schools. In most cases, however, when I visit and observe such "collaborations," I usually find the "same old wine in a new bottle"—the same preparation program, with a new name. That is, the university has chosen, paid, or solicited certain public schools (that university faculty have established personal ties with) to be the sites for student teaching, internships, and practicums; however, no real co-reform activities of mutual purpose, integrated teaching, and reciprocal influence are taking place. University personnel are not involved in the schools' decision making and planning, nor are the school people involved in decision making and planning for the curriculum and activities of the teacher education program. What happens is mutual *accommodation* to each other, not mutual *participation* in helping each other to improve. The result is that university faculty continue to go their own way, with their own agenda for scholarship, service, and teaching, and public school people continue to go their own way in their own classes, with occasional interruptions to supervise college interns and student teachers.

Despite all of the reports and the research and propositions espoused by such highly esteemed (and university-based) scholars as John Goodlad (1990), Linda Darling-Hammond (1994), and the Holmes Group (1995), the status quo of most teacher education programs remains the same. There are notable exceptions to this (see Darling-Hammond, 1994; Goodlad, 1996), but they are notable because they are the exceptions. I often ask myself, "Why is this so? Don't people understand the power of what could be accomplished for all our future teachers and all our public school students if research, planning, actions, and service could be democratically derived and implemented among the universities and public schools?" I think of the many public schools that have little resources in terms of time, outside knowledge, and personnel and could benefit hugely from having a university or college as a partner in their efforts. And I know that principals, teachers, parents, and students in public schools could dramatically improve teacher and school leadership preparation programs in higher education if they were invited to participate as equals.

The obstacles to co-reform, I think, reside more at the university then at the public school. The university is the dominant organization in terms of status and prestige and the appearance of expertise and knowledge. To be blunt, it's difficult for many university people to acknowledge that we don't have the answers to making educational life more robust and healthy in American public schools. We know our own specialty, and we know the results of our own controlled studies and subjects, but we don't know well what should be done in the day-to-day world of schools; it is beyond our control.

To put it another way, if the entire staff of a local teacher education school were to replace the staff of a local public school—from the administration to the faculty and support staff—the school probably would not be better off than before. Discipline issues, a fragmented purpose, irate parents, political infighting, and a range of poor to excellent teaching and learning practices would most likely be the result. In other words, school would look much the same. I also suspect that, likewise, a university teacher education program turned over to public school faculty and staff would not end up much different than before. Perhaps there would be greater emphasis on what to do and less on why, but there would be no greater overall cohesion in the program. My point is that both groups don't know enough about each other. The university could help dislodge this inertia by admitting it exists and listening more to public school people. In turn, public school personnel could become more open and gain other organizational and educational perspectives. So again, why is co-reform so hard to do? Because each of us, in our own institutional world, likes to have the answer for others. To admit that we don't know is to lower our guard and become more vulnerable. But it is also to create larger understanding and eventually become more powerful.

A first step toward co-reform is for universities and colleges—both administrators and faculty—to come clean and say that our mission, above all else, *is* teacher education. Therefore, scholarship, service, and teaching around the issues of improving our own teacher education programs should receive highest priority in terms of how we use university time, resources, incentives, and criteria for advancement. It would at least be a start.

─∿∿─ Governing for the Future

Historian Christopher Lasch observes that "the most serious threat to democracy, in our time, comes . . . from the decay or abandonment of public institutions in which citizens meet as equals" (1995, p. 19). Lasch argues further that professionalism has undermined democracy. It has created a "we" versus "they" attitude between professionals (lawyers, doctors, news reporters, educators, and so on) and other citizens. The professionals believe themselves to be superior—in rank and status—and condescendingly mediate and translate only what they believe laypersons are capable of learning. Thus professional bureaucracies and representative boards are formed to keep ordinary citizens in their place, removed from public institutions. Amy Gutmann's challenge (1987, p. 77) to public educators is that professionalism "should complete, not compete with" policies and governance structures that are congruent with the school as a democratic community.

In a previous book (Glickman, 1993), I addressed the dimensions of governance, schoolwide changes in teaching and learning, and action research as dimensions for internal site-based actions. Over the years, members of state boards of education, governor's offices, teachers' unions, superintendents, and school boards have asked me about what should be their role in regard to achieving school-based autonomy and decentralization. For example, should state departments, school districts, and teachers' unions have a function to serve in the localized efforts of individual schools, or should they simply be eliminated?

Since I've never been particularly concerned with regulatory agencies—other than with getting rules and regulations out of the way in schools that desire to develop and implement democratic practices—I had to think seriously about the questions of function, service, support, accountability, and control. Most of my work has been with schools where the principal and teachers want to be more inclusive, democratic, and purposeful and thus engender increased support among parents, students, and community members. Therefore I have a somewhat skewed vision of those who work in public schools. I have had only minimal contact with schools where educators were unaware of or resistant to improving education according to the democratic tenets of equality, liberty, and fraternity.

FIRST PRINCIPLES OF POLICY

All strong democracies grow from the inside, based on the initiative and will of people in a community to work for common aspirations. District and state policies must acknowledge that there are (1) schools with strong-willed people, which do not need external control, and (2) schools without the will to improve, which need to have greater structure and need to be held to certain standards as they work toward greater autonomy. In a just and equal society, how do external governments and organizations (school boards, state boards of education, and teachers' unions) allow democratic principles to blossom and at the same time respond to the developmental needs of school communities that range from curiosity about ongoing educational improvements to stiff resistance to them? The reasons for schools' not being democratic in operation and pedagogy are numerous—lack of awareness, complacency, cynicism, lack of administration support, and fear of change that will create disequilibrium, conflicts, and uncertainties, to name a few (Seeley, 1985). Districts, school boards, unions, and state departments traditionally have a regulatory responsibility to ensure that *all* students receive an adequate-quality education, regardless of the particular school they attend. There need to be clear policies for doing so.

The following is my attempt to address these developmental concerns by going back to the first principle of a democracy. *Such policies need to be developed with the same egalitarian spirit that they aim to achieve in the life of schools.* To do so, we will need a radical redefinition of accountability, to go along with a radical decentralization of responsibilities (Schlechty, 1990, 1997; Darling-Hammond, 1997; Sarason, 1996; Bauman, 1996). School boards will need to shift their roles to be more like educational Supreme Courts, deciding upon cases where democratic rights, responsibilities, and processes might have been violated. School districts and teachers' unions will need to provide services upon request to those schools already prepared to initiate democratic education, provide facilitation to those schools needing assistance to begin, and provide structure and regulations to those schools unaware of or resistant to change. All efforts—judicial, facilitative, and directive—will need to aim at shifting the responsibility for the local, internal operations of schools from the district and state to individual schools, to the local educators, students, parents, and community members. The role and voice of parents, more than any other group, should become the center of policies that will make democracy the serious business of schools (Sarason, 1994).

A POLICY SKETCH

Let me offer a policy sketch of ways that would recenter schools as democratic institutions.

1. *Schools that already have or wish to initiate being democratic and purposeful need special written agreements with their local school boards, teachers' unions, and state departments of education.* These should cover a minimum of three to six years and be renewable for like periods of time. Initiating schools need flexibility, authority, and responsibility for educational decision making; this will entail an agreed-upon degree of decentralization concerning curricula, staffing, assessment, staff development, schedules, and budgets. Schools can then be held responsible for results rather than for following set curricula, funding formulas, or other predetermined patterns and prescriptions. Furthermore, the written understandings should note that the school principal in such initiating schools will *not* be held solely accountable for results; rather, the onus of responsibility should reside with the democratic decision-making body and the school as a whole.

The principal is a part of, not distinct from, the participation and responsibility of the whole.

Written agreements should make clear that district officials, school board members, and teachers' union representatives will not intervene when the inevitable controversies about schoolwide change occur at the local-school level. Such controversy is part of the democratic dialectic and must be respected as the fuel that drives responsible decision making. When called upon by the school through its democratic body, the district and union should be ready to mediate between opposing factions, but they should not be relied upon to resolve the dispute. The resolution of disputed school decisions, within legal parameters and common democratic aspirations, must be the responsibility of the school. This is the only way that a school community can understand its power and responsibility and learn from its experiences, including its successes and its mistakes. Furthermore, there should be opportunities for teachers to form teams and to develop unique smaller schools within a larger physical school site. Such microschools—composed of faculty and students—should have the same defined understanding and approval from school councils, boards, and unions as the regular schools.

Substantial change is subject to the initial "implementation dip" (Fullan & Stiegelbaurer, 1991; Fullan, 1993). Unfreezing old ways of working, learning new roles, and trying out new patterns of education usually result in subsequent confusion and a decline in efficiency and effectiveness before consolidation and achievements become visible. Three to six years with a renewable clause allows schools to know that their work is for the long term, and beginning difficulties will not stop them.

2. *Initiating schools need access to like-minded schools.* Initiating schools should participate in multiyear collaborations within and across districts as members of democratic-school networks or peer coaching arrangements. There is a need for school people to visit and learn from one another about the ongoing struggles of this very human endeavor. Such networks already can be found in the United States in such organizations as the Coalition of Essential Schools (Sizer, 1996), the Accelerated Schools (Levin, 1991; Finnan, St. John, McCarthy, & Slovacek, 1995), the Success for All Schools (Slavin, 1996), the Annenberg Lead Schools, the New American School Design Teams, the Comer Schools (Comer and others, 1996), and the League of Professional Schools (Glickman, 1993). Districts, unions, and

regional and state agencies need to help create and multiply such networks rapidly, so that every initiating school in every school district can have "kinship" schools to work with in implementing democratic education. In this way, parents, teachers, principals, staff, and students can learn from one another, in cross-school settings, about the reality of such implementation efforts.

3.   *District central office personnel should serve initiating schools on an as-requested basis.* The existence of district positions and personnel need to be justified to initiating schools on the basis of the extent to which such schools can call upon them for assistance with facilitation, evaluation, planning, staff development, and curriculum development. The initiating schools should pay for such services, and if few initiating schools request the use of centralized services, then such services should be eliminated. (Please note that this is not an argument against "bureaucrats" or central office administrators, as if they are automatically negative. There are many districts with personnel of considerable expertise who offer excellent facilitation services for schools. Rather, it is simply to make clear that the *schools* are responsible for educating all students well, and the district and unions exist to *help* the schools do so. See Schlechty, 1990; Darling-Hammond, 1993.)

4.   *The strategic pressure-release valve of school choice will be needed for students, parents, and teachers who feel trapped in a no-win situation.* Parents, students, and teachers in large districts should have a choice, within set parameters, concerning which school they wish to attend or teach in. Small and rural districts need to form collaborations with one another to provide such choice. All such plans need to conform to legal parameters defining equitable racial and socioeconomic balance within schools and not be used to stratify and separate the student population. Such school choice provides an escape for students, faculty, or parents who cannot find satisfaction and comfort in the decisions and educational programs of their current school. When a student leaves one school for another, the funds to support that student should follow.

5.   *Any school in which less than 75 percent of parents and students have been satisfied with the current educational program over a three-year period should be placed on a one-year probationary status and directed to find better ways to meet the needs of dissatisfied parents and students.* I suggest a 25 percent level of student and parent dissatisfaction as a conservative measure for triggering probationary status.

The means for determining parent and student confidence could be a secret-ballot referendum every three years, or confidential exit interviews of students and parents who, during the previous years, chose to leave a particular school. The actual percentage and tally mechanisms for triggering probation should be determined by a representational group of board, district, school, parent, community, and student members. The reason that I argue that a 25 percent minority of dissatisfied students and parents should have such profound influence on the total work of the school is (1) to protect the rights of the minority to be heard and (2) to keep schools focused on their essential democratic charge to educate *all* students well. (Districts that are truly committed to all their students might choose as small a figure as 10 percent dissatisfied to trigger probation.) If after a one-year probation a second referendum indicates that the school still cannot meet the educational needs of a significant percentage of its students, then regardless of the individual performance of principals, teachers, and staff, the school should be abolished and re-created by the school board. The administration and faculty should be removed from the school, and a new faculty should be chosen by parent and district representatives. This means that seniority laws as currently advocated by teachers' unions should be changed so as not to protect the jobs of those who poorly serve students. After all, it does say in the Declaration of Independence that "whenever any form of government becomes destructive of these ends, it is the right of the people to alter or abolish it." All governmental professionals, including teachers, should embrace this rule in fulfilling their public obligations.

6.   *Every school, with its district, union, and school board, should have up to three years to develop its own governance methods, internal operations plans, and democratic teaching and learning.* There needs to be considerable discussion by those within the school (faculty, staff, students, parents, and community representatives) on how they will all be involved as equals, what their charter for decision making will look like, and how they will develop standards of educational practice to remain focused on education as democracy for all students. These are not simple matters. Initial agreements will need to be ratified by the people they affect and piloted on a yearly basis—for up to three years—before formal letters of understanding can be drafted with school boards, unions, and state departments of education.

OPENING NEW POSSIBILITIES

I've tried to explain in this essay that new policies for education as democracy need to be congruent with the key premises and principles of democracy (liberty, equality, fraternity) and the process of democracy (developed of, by, and for the people). Thus, details of democratic operations should *not* be imposed by mandates from external authorities. Such issues as equitable funding across all schools in a district or state should remain school district and state responsibilities. The greatest change will be in local school boards, which will become judiciary reviewers and monitors of democratic education. They will be the courts of first resort to ensure that principles of justice, equality, and democratic control are adhered to. Ultimate control over the pedagogical direction of the school (curricula, schedules, teaching materials, methods, and so on) should belong to parents and, at the secondary level, students.

Are such policies a threat to the current state of professionalism? Do they conflict with the notion that educators know best, and parents and the public should comply with their expert decisions? Yes, such policies are clearly a threat. Will they also support the alignment of educational practice with a belief in democracy as education? Clearly they will. As Sarason (1995) wrote, "educators could not be more realistic in the sense that once you take parent-community involvement seriously, life becomes more complicated, messy, and even more unpredictable than it was before. That life can *become* more interesting, exciting, less isolating, protective of the existence of the public schools, and potentially an aid to their improvement is a goal . . . called for: a vision that pulls us into the future" (p. 84).

PART THREE

On Getting Beyond

It appears that the perennial either-or debates about American conceptions of democracy, society, and education have become increasingly strident in their tone and level of dogmatism. These harsh battles tend to paralyze public schools from taking clear value stances. The result is "the shopping mall school" (Cohen, 1995), in which education tries to serve all masters, consumers, and special interests by taking a neutral, valueless stance and becomes afraid to promote any singular purpose. I argue in this part that public schools should be value-driven and have a singular, fundamental, absolute perspective of what they do to serve their obligation to democracy.

In the following essays I explain how such polemic battles—education to serve the economy versus education to enhance the quality of human life; monocultural versus multicultural views of American life; religion versus secular humanism; and state versus family controlled education—can be placed into perspective around democracy, participation, and human reason. Such a perspective is not affiliated with political parties or with liberal or conservative categories of thought—rather, it is affiliated with the constitutional hope of an educated populace.

⌇ Wealth and Welfare

As political scientist Charles Lindblom has noted, although "we . . . have tried the market in many of its possible forms, learning greatly from both its flaws and its merits . . . we have not yet tried democracy, only distant approaches to it" (1995, p. 684).

The president of a prestigious consulting firm that serves five hundred corporations told me of a recent project he had worked on with a well-known telecommunications company. He had helped the company's managers prepare to terminate, over a six-month period, 20 percent of the company's sixty-thousand-person workforce. He narrated that it was very difficult for middle managers to communicate this decision to their staffs, because the company had just had a record-breaking quarter in terms of profits, stockholder shares were up, and the CEO and various division presidents had been awarded large bonuses. I mentioned to him that, given such facts, I would be quite confused myself about the layoff decision. His explanation was that financial projections had shown that over the next several years, other, smaller companies would be competing in the same markets and would erode the company's current profit level. The company's payroll costs needed to be extensively trimmed for it to remain competitive. Thus, the necessity for the layoffs.

I admit to having more than a casual interest in this scenario. The president of the consulting firm is my eldest brother, and the company involved has been generous with gifts to education, specifically to support our university's collaborations with public schools. Furthermore, the CEO of this company has been a leading spokesperson for public education, frequently giving major addresses to business and community groups about the need to support public school reform to ensure a highly skilled, knowledge- and information-savvy workforce for the future.

THE SOCIAL EFFECTS OF
BOTTOM-LINE THINKING

This real-life example of what a company "had to do" to remain profitable troubled me greatly. (Of course, it troubled those who would lose their jobs far more.) Many corporate leaders, business analysts, and economists might dismiss my concern over these layoffs as the "bleeding heart" response of a mushy educator who doesn't understand the bottom line. Well, I think I do understand the corporate mentality and the bottom line. And, with all due respect, rarely does that bottom line have anything to do with the health and wealth of the workers in a company or the citizens in a democratic society. Instead, the bottom line has to do with profits. There is no personal conspiracy afoot of wealthy individuals on corporate boards who are attempting to deprive others of wealth, but often the actions of well-intentioned people merely doing their job as they understand it results in harm to society.

I'm not alone in my concern about how the "corporate bottom line" is understood in our society. Columnist Robert Reno wrote that "IBM has pulled off one of the most stunning corporate turn-arounds in American history. It took the distress of eliminating one-third of its employees (219,839) and threats of further pay cuts of up to 36 percent of workers at the same time the company is handing out nearly $6,000,000 in bonuses to its senior executives" (1995, p. 8A)

A dramatic example of bottom-line thinking can be found in the announcement of the Sara Lee Corporation's decision to cut nine thousand jobs: "There are no negatives. . . . [The layoffs] should translate into cost savings mounting up to $250,000,000 by fiscal 1997. . . .

This is an important step in sustaining Sara Lee's target of low double-digit earnings growth" ("Sara Lee Set to Trim up to 9,000 Positions," 1994, p. C1). A follow-up article about how this "no negatives" decision would affect people at two Sara Lee factories to be closed in Georgia provided this reaction from workers: "'Everyone cried,' said Willeen Raham, a 61-year-old sewing machine operator. 'I have no idea what I'll do. . . .' 'People have never had but one job, that's the saddest part,' said Paulette Combs as she and dozens of women left the plant" (Torpy, 1994, p. C1).

Taking on the CEOs and boards of directors of corporate America for what they are doing to their workers is not my main intent. After all, I plan to continue to work for and with them on issues related to education. My comments could easily be taken as the views of a left-wing, anticapitalist socialist—if not a downright communist! However, I am a capitalist. Between my wife (a school teacher) and myself (a university professor), my family has a very decent income of over $100,000 annually (which puts us in the top 4 percent of all wage earners in America). My father was a lifelong free-market entrepreneur, the president of a chain of small family-owned retail furniture stores in New England. As mentioned, my older brother is president of a business management consulting firm, and my younger brother manages a $300 million account for a leading computer firm. I have never been an employee of a large business. Any familiarity I have with that life comes from family, friends, neighbors, and officials I have served with on committees. However, I serve in many education-business partnerships, and on occasion I find myself in corporate boardrooms, planning educational priorities and programs. Usually I find a tension between educators and businesspeople in the language they use to discuss education. I like and enjoy the company of most business leaders, and I find myself repeatedly telling university colleagues of leftist leanings that such people are not arrogant, unfeeling, sinister individuals. For the most part, they are savvy, bright, personable, innovative, decent, and fun to be with. They are just like most successful public people in any area. Yet, because I do not participate in the intricacies of their day-to-day world and they do not participate in mine, when the big questions about the priorities and purpose of education arise, we often find ourselves talking past each other.

I do believe in capitalism, but capitalism regulated by a democratic conscience (see Lindblom, 1995; Chase, 1996; Kane, 1996; Sennott, 1996; Walker, 1996). For example, I don't think all aspects of socialism, in the sense that the land and wealth of a democracy should benefit all its people, are terrible ideas. Why should corporate leaders receive millions in bonuses while employees are laid off or take cuts in pay? Why shouldn't IBM, Sara Lee, or others make less profit and keep more hardworking Americans employed? Why should corporate heads, entertainers, and sports figures make millions of dollars a year while public servants (such as teachers, health care workers, police, and so on) make $20,000 or $30,000 a year? If money indicates value, then which of these does society value more? Why shouldn't individuals and corporations with wealth who have benefited greatly by American society pay more taxes than those with less wealth?

At times, I also have questions about the seriousness of the philanthropy of some large corporations. Some corporations have made arrangements with their local communities and states to pay little or no taxes and receive public services for free. They use services such as roads, schools, water, and discounted utility rates, then turn around and, through corporate giving, adopt the image of community benefactor. In reality, their gifts back to the community represent much less than what they should have paid in taxes in the first place. Over the past fifty years, individual income taxes have risen from 44 to 73 percent of total government revenue, while corporate taxes have fallen from 33 to 15 percent. If corporations had paid taxes at the same rate, there would be almost no federal deficit (Beatty, 1995).

The fact that American corporations play a major part in ruling America (both overtly and covertly) at public expense is not new. Historians argue that American capitalism always has been insensitive to the common people. Zinn says it is "a system driven by the one overriding motive of corporate profit and therefore unstable, unpredictable, and blind to human needs" (1980, p. 378). In the 1920s, a time of great prosperity for American business, nearly twenty-five thousand workers per year were killed on the job and one hundred thousand permanently disabled (p. 373). Business was indifferent to the health and welfare of workers and allowed unsafe and unchecked work conditions. It took moral outrage, activism, and, too often, bloodshed by ordinary men and women to change cruel child labor practices and to increase job safety and the wages of such groups as railroad, coal, steel, and garment workers.

Even legendary business leaders such as Henry Ford, J. P. Morgan, Henry Cabot Lodge, and John D. Rockefeller did not take action on their own to protect the welfare of their employees. The current trend of downsizing is another example of the bottom-line mentality, by which money and profits are more important than the welfare of workers. The current situation is in some ways no different. As financier Felix Rohatan wrote, "the institutional relationship created by the mutual loyalty of employers and employees in most American businesses has been badly frayed . . . replaced by a combination of fear for the future and a cynicism for the present as a broad proportion of working people see themselves as temporary assets to be hired or fired to 'protect the bottom line' and 'create shareholder wealth'" (quoted in Reno, 1995, p. 8A).

For the past twenty years, the social health of America has declined as the economy has improved. Marc Miringou, director of a Fordham University study on the social health of America, wrote, "We really have to . . . reassess this notion that the gross domestic product . . . is going to produce improvements in the quality of life" (quoted in Landsberg, 1995).

Now, before public servants and union members begin applauding my stance, I can make similar accusations regarding the self-serving hierarchies that have been built around the greed of union leaders. The United States also has a history of manipulation by union heads and insensitivity to union members. To summarize, free-market capitalism is not intrinsically good. It does not automatically do good work; business attends to the bottom line first. The result of all this is that there is a constant, often unspoken tension between educators and the corporate world concerning who has clearer insights about the purpose of education.

WHO SERVES WHOM?

The old division between Hamiltonian and Jeffersonian conceptions of American democracy is apparent in the confusion among educators and businesses over the aim of education. Business sees education as serving the economy. Businesspeople stress the importance of job preparation, economic competitiveness, the global economy, and free-market capitalism and the role of education in promoting them. Virtually all of the highly publicized national reports on education since 1983 have stressed workforce preparation and the global economy as the rationale for why we need to reform education (National Commission on Excellence in Education, 1983; McMannon, 1995). According to these reports, education for democracy has to do with educating students for their role in the economy. When they mention civic education, they mean learning about the Constitution and American history, not learning how to question and redefine "liberty" and "justice and equality for all." The unquestioned assumption by business is that the material life is defined by a high income and consumption. In other words, the material life is the life successful businesspeople live, and they want the younger generation to learn how to live it as well as they do, or better. Thus, the economic lament is that for the first time, the next generation of Americans may not make as much income (and thus will consume less) than the previous generation.

Educators tend to be less concerned with economic success. They see the role of education as providing resources and settings for students to apply their knowledge, participate, and gain greater degrees of autonomy, free expression, and choice. They see schooling as a tool to help students become valued citizens who can define their own good life. Work is seen as a means to the higher ends of greater individual liberty, choices, and involvement. Thus, education does not exist to prepare people for work; work is to be sought as a means to a secure life, which helps people continue to learn and grow individually and together. This is why so many educators are put off by businesspeople. As Lasch wrote, "the market . . . puts an almost irresistible pressure on every activity to justify itself in the only terms it recognizes: to become a business proposition. . . . Inexorably it remodels every institution in its own image" (1995, p. 98). Talk about students as "customers" and education as a "product" reduces education to an economic engine for the nation. These words ignore the greater purposes of education—realizing free expression, supporting critical thinking, and aiding students in the pursuit of their own truths.

Now, the reason why such a gap exists between the two groups in their thinking about the fundamental purpose of education is because the lives of their members are so different. Educators did not emphasize money, income, and consumption in their choice of a career. When they became public servants, they knowingly gave up the possibility of attaining great wealth. Teaching students—for limited pay and in a confined, mentally stimulating but exhausting place—was their choice. (Admittedly, in some lower-income communities educators enjoy greater income and flexibility than many others in the population.) Businesspeople, on the other hand, chose careers that gave them the opportunity to attain much greater status and income. Business success is measured in terms of income, status, advanced responsibilities, and, for many people, consumption. Since everyone wishes to remake the world in his or her own image, successful businesspeople want educators to educate students to be more like themselves, and successful educators want students to be more like themselves. Surprisingly, although each group's goals for education are very different, much of the educational content and processes that support those differing goals are the same. Although the purposes are different, the processes are quite similar. This is where common agendas around educational reform as democratic learning—for life and for work—can be found.

AN EDUCATIONAL AGENDA FOR WORK— LESSONS FROM CORPORATE AMERICA

Personnel directors from large corporations told soon-to-be college graduates that they need not worry about whether they had selected the right major for gaining an entry-level job. Whether it was to be a career in financing, sales, science, service, manufacturing, or communication, the directors noted that they were seeking the same competencies of graduates. They wanted students who demonstrated

- Basic competence in whatever subjects or majors they had studied
- Good interpersonal skills
- Good communication skills, both verbal and written
- Resourcefulness and initiative
- Knowing where and how to find information
- Literacy in technology, particularly in computer usage
- Familiarity with foreign languages

As a friend of mine who heads an international sales division said, "We are looking for people who can solve, rather than make problems. People who can internalize, produce, communicate, and create knowledge with others."

In needs assessment sessions I have attended with corporate CEOs and heads of divisions of human resources, they have identified the optimal educational experiences that will ensure that their employees are well prepared to participate in their organizations:

- Active, participatory learning
- Cooperative learning and group brainstorming
- Seminars with much time for questions, answers, and discussions
- Frequent time for application and experimentation in a threat-free, supportive environment
- Chances for actual demonstrations of learning through field applications

This listing of essential experiences for learning is virtually identical to the pedagogy of democracy.

Furthermore, a two-year study of workplace strategies of one thousand American companies found that companies using strategies of employee participation had the greatest long-term profits. In such organizations, "employees were treated as assets to be developed rather than costs to be cut" (Genasci, 1995b, p. 8A). Such strategies involved

- Achieving specific innovations and improvements by empowering employees to make decisions
- Cooperating with unions in organizational planning and change
- Committing to continuing education for all employees, on company time

These "participatory" companies outperformed the others in employer and employee satisfaction, production efficiency, product quality, and profits.

If one studies closely the underlying message of business gurus such as Drucker, Deming, Peters, Covey, and Ouichi and their best-selling books, one will find that the key to successful business is successful workers who are invited to be part of a democratic workplace. The current terms *quality management, transformational business,* and *reinventing corporations* are mostly restatements of an old notion, that people can govern and manage themselves when treated as equals and as curious, competent, and resourceful persons capable of participating with others in making wise decisions. So even from the bottom-line view, when given support, time, and resources, democracy of, by, and with workers works.

So although a gap remains between their ultimate purpose, there is a strong alliance between reform-minded businesspeople and educators in demanding changes in public education processes and structures; both want more active learning by students and structural changes in schedules and technology to increase flexibility for students and teachers (Hartoonian & VanScotter, 1996). This is why such strange political bedfellows as conservative free marketers stand side by side with social liberals in their basic exhortation that schools as they currently exist—in pedagogy and structure—don't support the type of students, either as economic "products" or as free thinkers, needed in the future (Kincheloe, 1995; Lugg & Dentith, 1996).

But before these groups shake hands over their agreement concerning the need for new processes and content, the divisive issue of who serves whom must be resolved. It is still a most important and potentially contentious issue. It has wide implications for the scope of curricula, the required courses, the nature of student experiences, and the measured results of education.

If education is for freedom in a democracy—for ensuring one's own life, liberty, and pursuit of happiness and protecting the same for other citizens—and not mainly career preparation, then the curriculum needs to be broad-based, and students should not be made to select particular, tracked career options. Work experience in business and the public sector should support and reinforce students' general academic competence, communications skills, critical thinking, and associative learning. Curriculum, courses, concentrations, and projects should not prepare students for particular jobs or careers; rather, they should be experiences that teach students how to continue to learn and how to expand choices about the good life. On the other hand, if education is to be mainly economic preparation, then the curriculum needs to be narrowly focused on career preparation, with concentrated majors and predetermined course routes, levels, or tracks. Job experience and community experiences are then used as training to do the specific type of work that one might later pursue.

RETURNING TO A LIBERAL EDUCATION

I believe that all public compulsory education in America should be a general education, not one that sorts students into college or vocational tracks.[1] As of today, it is compulsory for most children to attend public schools until age sixteen. The public responsibility should be to provide an education for all citizens that equips them to learn how to participate, think, and make future choices among various notions of the good life. More specific choices regarding higher education and careers should come after the age of sixteen and need not be provided exclusively by public schools. If after the age of sixteen a student wishes to move directly into a specific career training program, an apprenticeship, or an institution of higher education, it should be the job of the educational system of local communities and the state to enable such pursuits. Why should a student stay in school after age sixteen to receive a high school diploma if he or she has and is ready to pursue more specific educational or career goals?

Education that is compulsory should be general. An adaption of Goodlad's proposal (1984, p. 287) of a general curriculum, with specific content and details left to the local educators, parents, community members, and students, appears quite sensible. Each student would divide his or her total school time as follows among the content domains of a general education:

- Up to 18 percent in literature and language
- Up to 18 percent in mathematics, science, and technology
- Up to 15 percent in social studies
- Up to 15 percent in the arts
- Up to 15 percent in career awareness and public service activities, which should support learning in the above four areas
- Up to 10 percent in physical education
- The remaining 10 percent or more in student-selected areas of special interest

The core learnings for all students would be the same, but the rate and speed of progress would vary among individuals. Learning in any area could be extended, accelerated, or deepened through mutual arrangements between students and their teachers. Students nearing the age at which attendance is no longer compulsory would need to meet community-approved standards of demonstrated performance prior to further career training or higher education pursuits.

What is different about this proposal from current public school curricula is that it does not include job training. Instead, there would be career awareness sessions and opportunities for practicums, internships, and community and work projects as part of—rather than apart from—the core general education. There would not be academic teachers and vocational teachers. There would be teachers with various expertise and strengths working together to provide a general education for all students.[2]

What this boils down to, in my mind, is that society should not compel students to attend school merely to prepare them for jobs. While students are being educated for the public (that is, while they are attending public school), the aim of their education should be the original definition of liberal arts, "to learn to be free." A curriculum that balances the five domains of a general education and allows adequate daily time for individual and group pursuits based on personal interests, inclinations, and abilities is most appropriate to fostering the ideas of a good life and its many manifestations.

Columnist Ellen Goodman wrote about a 1995 conference on "the new economic equation," attended by business, government, and academic leaders. Many of these financially and professionally successful people talked candidly about a void in their lives, about how the pressures of new technologies and the constant desire for more wealth and more acquisitions had put their work lives in direct opposition to the rest of their lives. What was revealing about such a discussion was the admittance that "after all, for the most part concerns about family, about community, about the good life, are set outside the margins when we talk about the economy" (p. 10a).

Another way of rethinking the issue of the economy and human welfare can be found in a statement from U.S. Labor Secretary Robert B. Reich: "The core meaning of competitiveness has got to be improved living standards for Americans. . . . If we have economic growth and most Americans don't enjoy it, we're not succeeding as an economy" (quoted in Swoboda, 1994, p. 87).

There is much for our students to learn to do. Perhaps one reason that we haven't dealt squarely with the democratic purpose of public education is that we as adults fear that by doing so, our children might learn to change the margins of "living the good life" and put our current criteria to shame.

Notes

1. In emphasizing a general education rather than a focus on college or vocations, it is important to note that "since the 1950s, only around 30 percent

of all jobs have required a four-year college degree and only 20 percent of all employment has been in the professional ranks. These ratios are not predicted to change in the future" (Gray, 1996, p. 530).

2. For details about such staffing arrangements to provide an integrated, general education, see Sizer (1984, 1992, 1996), Meier (1995), and Kincheloe (1995).

~~ Isms and Reasons

In 1787, in a speech before the final session of the Constitutional Convention, Benjamin Franklin said, "Most men, indeed, as well as most sects . . . think themselves in possession of all truth, and that wherever others differ from them, it is so far error. . . . But, though many private persons think almost as highly of their own infallibility as of that of their sect, few express it so naturally as a certain [person who said] 'But I meet with nobody but myself that is *always* in the right'" (quoted in Ravitch & Thernstrom, 1992, p. 110).

Fundamentalism, multiculturalism, humanism, postmodernism, empiricism, liberalism, conservatism—all are examples of Franklin's observation about the penchant for individuals and groups to categorize human thought into "possessors of all truth" and those who "so far error." The danger of such schools of thought about the world, human nature, society, and knowledge is that they force individuals to take sides and make it easy intellectually to define one's "thought friends" and "thought enemies." Taking a position because it passes the test of a particular group's thinking—and thereby not having to consider the rationale and merits of opposing views—is a form of tyranny. It might be more instructive to admit that rarely does an individual privately think according to a singular line of reasoning. Press hard, and self-described liberals will admit to some conservative views, religious fundamentalists to secular humanist views, Western monoculturalists to multiculturalist views, postmodernists to empiricist views, and so on. Education for freedom of thought does not come prepackaged in boxes of group "isms" but in individual exploration of competing and collaborating ideas.

WESTERN VERSUS MULTICULTURAL VALUES

Jefferson had misgivings about opening America to non-English-speaking and non-northern-European immigrants (as if America did not already contain numerous people not of European origin—a convenient oversight on Jefferson's part). His fear was that those not raised in the Western tradition of the Enlightenment, which stressed human reason and law, would become a majority of U.S. citizens and turn the country into a theocracy, monarchy, or other form of totalitarian state. His concern that unrestricted immigration of people steeped in different traditions of governance would result in the subversion of democracy was not an unreasonable fear, and neither is it today. Yet, Jefferson argued vehemently that religious tolerance, freedom of speech, and the protection of those who attacked democratic governance were essential to a democracy (see Jefferson's retort to the Sedition Act of 1798, quoted in Randall, 1993, pp. 533–534).

So, on the one hand, Jefferson advocated for a monocultural perspective, in which citizens would accept a belief in reason, law, and democracy; and on the other hand, he advocated for a multicultural perspective, in which citizens would accept contrary opinions, ideas, and even heresies about the society he was shaping. To complicate matters more, Jefferson saw no contradictions between these two perspectives but saw them as vital to each other.

It is in today's arguments by Western monoculturalists and multiculturalists that the two appear to be irreconcilable. The Western monoculturalists believe that there is a single, significant body of magnificent (Western) literature, ideas, facts, and thoughts—written mostly by white, European men—that must be the core curriculum for all American students (Bennett, 1995; Hirsch, 1996; Henry, 1994). All youngsters should know these parables, stories, histories, and heroes of the Western, European, and American tradition in order to further promote a common culture among all existent and future U.S. citizens. The multiculturalists retort that the Western monocultural canon is an artificial, arbitrary concept fostered by the ruling elite to defend their status as the only "true Americans," to assimilate others into "their" way of thinking, and to keep racial, ethnic, and gender minorities and immigrants who don't assimilate second-class citizens (not one of "us" but "them"). The multiculturalists argue that an inclusive curriculum that gives attention to the contribution of all minority groups, that accepts and supports diverse customs and languages and demythologizes the "melting pot" version of American history, is essential for all students to value their own unique histories and to learn to accept others in an equal society (Countryman, 1996; Banks, 1994; Zinn, 1980; Timm, 1996).

What the arguments come down to is how to answer these questions: What are American cultural values? How should American education be oriented culturally? My answer is that American democracy has been, and always will be, an expansion and contraction of particular cultures, values, and histories; the unity of a plurality of people around a common idea is its essence *("e pluribus unum")*. The eternal contradictions of different groups are subsumed under a greater ideal of listening, reasoning, and understanding. This gives voice and influence to Americans from all cultures, wherever they come from and whoever they are, as long as individuals of one culture do not negate, suppress, or hurt individuals of other cultures.

There is truth to the Western monoculturalists' version of American history as the great melting pot. There are many individuals who arrived penniless from other countries, struggled and ultimately found acceptance and encouragement, adopted Western language, thoughts, and costumes, and succeeded astonishingly in America. Such success stories can be found among newly arrived immigrants as well as among second- or third-generation Americans, and they can be found among members of oppressed minority groups and Native Americans. Monoculturalists can cite large numbers of such individuals who didn't just melt into the pot but became the chiefs. Such persons can be found in academia, literature, sports, entertainment, arts, and finance. However, there is another story of America that supports the multiculturalist version. There are many persons in America from various cultures, races, and traditions who have been sold a bill of goods about equality in America. Their own language, heritage, and customs have been suppressed. Even when individuals opted to leave their old ways and melt into the pot, the pot was nowhere to be found. What they received was not justice and equality but a life filled with restrictions, boundaries, poverty, and discrimination. They were clearly told by those who had power, status, and influence in America that they did not belong. What makes these two truths of America so poignant is that individuals can be found from the same immigrant, minority, or traditionally discriminated against cultures to prove both points (Schlesinger, 1992; Lipset, 1996).

So, what is a reasonable perspective? Should America be monocultural or multicultural? Is it a country of individual and group access to success or a nation of unmitigated exploitation? Which truth should we teach?

Let's be clear. America was never discovered. Native people had lived here since ancient times. Africans were here before the Pilgrims. The United States of America was formed officially as a pluralistic society—that is why many of the Western European settlers came to America, for religious and cultural freedom. From the beginning there were Native Americans, French, English, Spanish, Africans, Italians, Indians, and Asians. Some chose to be in America of their own free will, some did not. But they all had a significant influence on the history of the country and continue to influence America today. It would seem that honesty about America is the best education. All American children need to learn the fullest story of America—multiculturalism is the larger set. Multiculturalism includes the dominant influence of Western thought on its political institutions, economic system, and expansions. But as historian Zinn notes, "the past does not come only. . . from the point of view of government, conquerors, diplomats, leaders" (1980, p. 9) but also from the point of ordinary people, struggling groups, and leaders of resistance movements. All of American history is worth knowing, both its successes and its failures—"the dream," "the melting pot," "the mosaic," "the quilt."

Jefferson saw no contradictions in a monocultural society's having a pluralistic perspective, or in expecting immigrants to readily adapt to both. Where Jefferson erred was in thinking that freedom, justice, and equality reside in only one region, one gender, and one culture. History has proved him wrong. But more important, he was right that democracy—in its variety and complexity—is the overriding unifying principle; all else is secondary. The Western canon is multicultural in that, in its democratic traditions, it respects multiple ways of reasoning and multiple means of achieving individual expression. As such, we uncover a greater appreciation of what we all can contribute to and resolve among one another. As Massaro reminds us, if we understand that multiculturalism in itself is a Western concept, there are no irreconcilable differences and no contradictions (1993, p. 145). Cornell West elaborates: "The greatest experiment, as we know, began in 1776. . . . It didn't apply to white men who had no property. It didn't apply to women. It didn't apply to slaves. . . . But that is not solely the point. It is in part the point. But it is not fully the point. The courageous attempt to build a democracy experiment in which the uniqueness of each and every one of us, the sanctity of each and every one of us who has been made equal in the eyes of God becomes at least possible" (1993, p. 8).

The best promotion of democracy is not to fear those who come from different traditions but to educate all about how such differences—when tolerated and supported—can make a more, not less, democratic nation.

POSTMODERNIST VERSUS EMPIRICAL THOUGHT

First, I must admit that this issue does not appear to affect the nature of everyday relations among people or within educational institutions, despite what many academic essays, books, reviews, and editorials indicate (Lasch, 1995, p. 176). For one not familiar with this literature, let me explain what this debate is about.

Knowledge, from the time of Descartes, developed from a certain way of human reasoning defined as scientific. This meant empirical investigation, observation, linear causal relations, and holding a distance between researcher and subject as object. Therefore, what came to be known as "true" was detached from subjectivity, intuition, emotion, immediate experience, and interpersonal relationships. Objective and quantifiable methods of science have influenced virtually all disciplines: literature, philosophy, history, anthropology, psychology, sociology, physics, and mathematics. According to the postmodernist view, such unquestioned beliefs about science and empiricism as the superior basis for knowledge have validated an authoritarian mask of power and ruled out other methods of knowledge construction as inferior. This empirical, objective way of knowing represents a white, European, male model of the world, and it denies and curtails the thoughts of others. Therefore, according to the postmodernist, such scientific and "logical" research and texts need to be analyzed for the hidden power and control that the empiricists hold over others. Who the knower is and why he or she uses certain language, methods, investigations, and results is more important than the investigation and results themselves. Postmodernism as a movement consists of a loose grouping of writers, artists, advocates, and scholars who attempt to push beyond mainstream and accepted discourse, theories, investigations, communication, and boundaries. They are united in their rejection of any grand theory that universally explains the world and tries to rule supreme.

Postmodernists argue that all forms of knowing have equal legitimacy, all expressions are acceptable forms of voice, and there are no hierarchies of wisdom. Thus, a noted literary postmodernist can state that any ten words—picked at random—can be a poem. Another postmodernist states that no book can be read for what is written but instead must be "read" for what is omitted. Another claims that all seminal thinkers of any period should not be understood by their public speeches, writings, or novels but need to be deconstructed according to their personal behaviors and attitudes toward gender, race, class, and sexuality. Another argues that subjective intuition—not explainable or verifiable to others—is as clear a form of knowledge as logical reason.

Analytical, scientific thought clashing with postmodernist thought in the forms of learning, communication, and decision making has major import to the concept of education in a democracy. If all forms of knowledge are appropriate, how does a community make decisions? If there are no boundaries or criteria for communication, how do people talk or communicate with one another? If hidden, personal motives are more important to the message than the message itself, what and who can we believe? Ultimately, what ways of knowing are to be taught in public schools and learned by students? How does one educate between the opposite poles of believing in scientific, empirical knowledge as superior versus seeing multiple, nonhierarchical, subjective knowledge as being of greater legitimacy?

I believe that the postmodernists are right to an extent. For example, before I, as the writer of this book, try to explain how I would resolve this issue, it might be helpful, or at least of interest, to know about me, my life—my own personal context. I learned as a child to read from left to right, to form complete sentences, and to use logical arguments to convince others of my point of view. (The reader has probably by now uncovered that my childhood learning was not a complete success.) Books were and continue to be a rich source of information, but I have come to increasingly value firsthand experience. My preparation in young adulthood for teaching was in school, home, and community settings, where I was a member of a minority group. My education included sensitivity training in racial, gender, and interpersonal relations. I learned that people use different forms of personal and cultural expression (tone, emotion, nonverbal behaviors, and storytelling to make significant points).

I partially agree with the postmodernists. I believe that analytical, causal, objective reasoning does limit discourse, precludes certain discussions, and puts artificial boundaries on what should be examined and discussed. Insight, intuition, care, anger, love, hate, and faith are forms of human knowledge that need to gain legitimacy in human discourse. Yet, I also partially agree with Western rational empiricists— those white, European, male, scientific traditionalists who believe that all forms of communication must have order and grand rules if they are to be understood among people. I, as the receiver of a communication, need to understand, at least in part, what you are expressing— whether through reason, pictures, emotion, or presence—*if* the intent is to find and decide upon a common range of actions that will better us all. If I cannot understand and cannot find a way to understand what someone else is expressing, then I am lost and cannot learn. Thus, if the intent of the expression is to find commonality, then I need to understand you. If your expression is not meant to communicate, then it will silence me, make me turn away, make me angry or sad, or make me act out of compliance. Therefore, you and I must both have the logical and analytical skills to explain, follow, and understand each other.

The common ground of a democracy are those areas in which all of us—knowers and learners—can contribute our opinions and beliefs, in whatever form or manner. We as a group of individuals must develop a criteria of better knowledge and practice—not absolute truth—that "makes sense" and has a logical probability of improving the general welfare of all. (Examples of such criteria for educational decisions are provided in the essay "Constitutional Hope for Education.") Without common analysis and hierarchies of better rationales and solutions arrived through human reasoning, we have no way of collectively acting and thus no higher purpose than individual preference. As the feminist scholar Seyla Benhabib wrote, "post-modernism can teach us the theoretical and political traps of why utopias and foundational thinking can go wrong, but it should not lead to a retreat from utopia altogether" (1992, p. 230).

With such a view of common discourse, I can argue that ten random words do not make a poem for me, and I can argue that the children's novel *Little Tree* gives insights about universal human decency, even though it was written by an individual known to be a narrow-minded bigot (Carter, 1976). I can be secure in knowing that there are facts that can be objectively and observably known, such as the fact that horrible atrocities have occurred in Germany, America, Russia, and Africa; such historic truths cannot be dismissed as subjective rendering of opinions that people simply made up. I do not apologize for my Western thought processes that seek logic, explanations, and reasons. They are a part of how I think, what I believe, and how I reason. In turn, if others think and act differently from me, they need not apologize either. What postmodernism has contributed to the issue of education is the concept of giving back to the victims their dialect (Benhabib, 1992, Chapter 4). But giving back to people who have been omitted from the decisions of the past the right to express themselves in whatever manner they choose cannot be achieved by taking away the same right from others.

We all must be prepared to help others understand us by giving the reasons behind our insights and thoughts. Benjamin Barber (1992, Chapter 4; 1995, personal communication) draws a distinction between *reasoning* (engaging in linear, analytical thought) and *giving reasons* (explaining why one thinks as one does). The point is that reasoning does not have to be the only way of constructing knowledge, but "giving reasons" for one's knowledge construction is imperative for democratic decision making. Every expression of a desire to communicate and every attempt to understand one another, no matter by what form, adds to a democratic future.

⎯⎳⎯ Religion, Secular Humanism, and Geese

Most educators, parents, citizens, school board members, politicians, and casual newspaper readers are aware of the debate between religion and secular humanism (Nord, 1995; Carter, 1993). One group, identified as the secular humanists, says that public education and religion should never be mixed—all prayer, religious celebrations, religious censorship of books, religious learning materials, and teaching of religious values should be avoided in schools at all costs. The other group, identified as religious fundamentalists, argue that America is a Christian nation and that Christian values are essential for a moral, ethical, and responsible society. They believe that religious values have been systematically purged from our nation by secular humanists and that this has led to a valueless and irresponsible society. They contend that religious values need to be returned to the school in the form of prayer, teaching of Christian beliefs, censorship of non-Christian and "deviant" lifestyles, and teaching abstinence from sexual intercourse before marriage. Any information about abortion, contraception, and the contracting of sexually transmitted diseases such as AIDS should not be taught to students. The highly charged debate between religionists and secularists appears to take no prisoners.

It has resulted in public protests, much litigation, and, at times, violence. What I wish to do here is to address this issue in the larger context of democracy as education, in order to find solutions to such polarized issues *within our schools.* (I'm afraid that the polarized debates will continue to rage within society as a whole over abortion, family values, and acceptable lifestyles.)

Public education is a secular, humanist institution, and no pejoratives are implied in this statement. All American democratic institutions are nonsectarian, secular, and humanist, from the federal treasury to the post office and the National Park Service. The United States was founded by many who had fled from religious persecution in their homeland. The citizens of each state agreed, when they ratified the Constitution, to endorse the concept of religious toleration and forswear any notion of establishing an official state religion. All religions and all forms of belief, from monotheism to deism to agnosticism to atheism, were not just to be tolerated but also allowed to flourish according to their own ability to influence the minds and habits of men and women. American democracy was to have no role in supporting, negating, or excluding particular religions or religious beliefs. Jefferson wrote that "the rights of conscience we [as individuals] never submitted, we could not submit. We are answerable for them to our [own] God. The legitimate powers of government extend to such acts as are injurious to others. But it does me no injury for my neighbor to say there are twenty gods, or no God. It neither picks my pocket nor breaks my leg" (quoted in Peterson, 1975, p. 209).

Jefferson wrote that government sponsorship of religion in other nations had created intolerance and harm to others of dissimilar religious (or nonreligious) persuasions, and such support of any one religion would stifle the growth of a society as a whole. Instead, a democracy must allow for divergent beliefs of conscience so that decisions about the betterment of society to further guarantee freedom and liberty would be based on "reason and free inquiry . . . the only effectual agents against error" (p. 211).

The words of the Declaration of Independence, the Bill of Rights and the Constitution, and the *Federalist* papers indicate no hostility toward religion, simply the firm belief that all forms of religion and spirituality should be protected by making no law that establishes one form in favor of others. Therefore, democratic society is *secular* in that no one version of God or religion is officially sanctioned, and it is *humanist* in that it is, as Lincoln said at Gettysburg, "of the people, by the people, for the people." In a democracy, the people—not God (or God's representatives on earth)—make the decisions about life and community.

I would agree with religious moralists such as Stephen Carter that as a contemporary society we have taken the U.S. Constitution and various court rulings on the separation of church and state to mean we have the right to belittle and repress religious beliefs in public discussions about policies, values, and ethical behaviors. However, there is nothing in the courts' decisions that promotes or allows repression of religion, and for government agents to do so is as unconstitutional as it is to advance religion (Dayton, 1995). We have tended to ignore and not teach the history and contributions—both positive and negative—of various forms of religious beliefs, groups, and organizations. This avoidance is easily understandable. Since religion is a personal and sacred matter, to teach and explore carefully the role of religions puts many a teacher on uncertain and defensive ground.

How should our secular humanist society deal with this issue? Constitutionally, schools may not conduct prayer, celebrate any religion, or circumscribe curricula according to religious beliefs (see Peck, 1992, Chapter 13). To do so would be to make public education the state's agent for sponsorship of a state religion. This clearly is wrong. Some religious advocates argue that secular humanism is a religion with the same standing as Catholicism, Protestantism, Hinduism, Judaism, and Islam and that the state is sponsoring it and excluding all others. This argument is ridiculous in its circular reasoning. Such reasoning would suggest that any set of beliefs not rooted in religion are in fact religious. This would make any utterance religion. Some individuals who call themselves secular humanists ascribe to a firm disbelief in religion and have a dogmatic bent to get rid of all religions, but by definition, secular humanists in America are all U.S. citizens, including both those with and those without a fervent attachment to a particular religion. We are all secular humanists, because the Constitution gives the power to rule our society to humans.

Individuals do not leave their personal convictions and religious beliefs behind when they enter a schoolhouse, school board office, or state policymaking committee meeting. To say that people's religious and spiritual values should not influence their conception of a good society and good education is to leave men and women with a limited basis for reasoning with one another. If I am a devout Muslim, Jew, Christian, or Hindu, what I believe to be proper, good, and moral will, most hopefully, be directly tied to my religious beliefs. In a secular democracy, I need not pretend differently. Discussions about such issues as what should be taught in school, what should be the rules of conduct and civility, and what should be the guiding morals and values of a secular society will naturally be informed by the participants' spiritual beliefs. I have the same right as anyone else, of different religious beliefs or nonreligious beliefs, to argue my opinion and attempt to influence others. After all, I am who I am, and a democracy must protect the individual right of free expression. Conceptions of moral life are not exclusively the province of those with deeply held religious beliefs or those without religious beliefs; they are held by all. Therefore, issues concerning curricula, abstinence-based sex education, and censorship of materials can freely be debated according to people's individual religious convictions, but religious convictions themselves cannot be the basis for state endorsement or support of particular educational materials, programs, or operations.

What does all this mean? First, pragmatically speaking, it means that unless the Constitution is amended, decisions in a school or district that smack of state endorsement of a particular religion or set of religious beliefs will be repeatedly overturned by the courts. Second, it means that since every citizen is a member of our secular humanist society, all decisions must be formed through the invitations and involvement of all citizens, across the entire spectrum of religious and spiritual orientations. And third, all censorship of information must be challenged by secular criteria. Society must teach children the most correct and complete information; it must not knowingly teach information that is incomplete or incorrect, and it must not withhold information. As Jefferson envisioned it, if our democracy is to be perpetuated, education must "diffuse knowledge more generally through the mass of the people" (quoted in Peterson, 1975, p. 193). Therefore, all knowledge that is accepted as scientifically true and is within the capability of students to understand it must be taught. This means that no public school student should be denied the opportunity, at a developmentally appropriate age, to learn about the latest findings about pregnancy, sexually transmitted diseases, abortion, and birth control or be deprived of the latest medical opinions about homosexuality as normal rather than deviant behavior. Likewise, all public school students should be taught that there are debatable issues in history (for example, did Columbus "discover" America? Was he a hero, a villain, or both? From whose perspective?) and that there are varying perspectives according to different religious beliefs about the creation of life. Teachers should not present to students *as truth* ideas or theories about the world that have no grounding in the scientific investigations of secular humanism—the accumulation of findings from studies of humans, by humans, for humans.

So long as decisions by educators, parents, and citizens about curricular scope and sequence adhere to the criteria of (1) no endorsement of religion, (2) decision-making processes that encourage the airing of all opinions and beliefs and do not allow a minority to impose its views on the majority, and (3) the teaching only of known truth and not of error, they will be upheld by the courts as constitutional (Massaro 1993, p. 91). As long as they have an educational rationale and are not arbitrary or capricious, decisions by local educators and citizens on school matters will be left alone.

So when all is said and done, the battle between secular humanism and religion is not what it often appears to be. It is a false battle. It is not a battle of nonreligious groups of people against religious groups of people. It is, instead, a battle over whether all citizens, regardless of their beliefs, will contribute to the market of ideas about society, school, and education so that human resolutions can occur. It is in the marketplace of ideas that the debates must be resolved and answered by men and women, not by God. An American democracy can never be a theocracy.

—∿—

At this moment, I am writing about religion and secular humanism in a quiet place. There are no planes to catch, no meetings to attend, and no phones to answer. I look outside and see the leaves changing to the deep fall colors of red and orange. Suddenly I hear the sound of cackling voices, and I look upward. Canada geese fill the sky on their flight southward. I enjoy moments like this: alone, silent, and in wonderment. These times remind me that I am a small part of a larger life of birth, growth, and death. Whether I call these moments prayer, meditation, or reflection are not important. I don't know which they are, nor do I particularly care. We all need time to pause and think about the world and where our life fits. Most of us—whether we are deeply religious or spiritual or not—seek such times. We know that the material world as it now exists is not right. It entices us to value what we don't want to value; it encourages us to be more hedonistic, aggressive, and self-absorbed than what we know to be right. We also know that we either actively or passively pass such corruptions on to our young.

At these quiet times, looking and listening to the geese, knowing that the moral, natural, spiritual, and social world is beyond my ability to control and that I am insignificant in the total scheme of history, events, and the rhythm of the universe, I am better able to think about what I am and what I want to be. Can I make a dent in defining and forging a better world? I hope so, but I don't think it will be done through making grand speeches, attending "important" meetings, or writing articles and books. Instead, I believe a better world is made in the small, everyday interactions among and with people. These thoughts are not new to me, but they become clearer, deeper, and more important as I grow older and see others pass through this world. All great religious and spiritual leaders have spoken eloquently about the need to find places and times to step away from the world as it now is in order to find a greater meaning for living a virtuous life.

I am troubled that we haven't acknowledged that there is a common core of virtue for American education, rooted in religious, spiritual, and private conscience. All of us espouse such beliefs as the need to love not only our own family and personal friends but to love all our fellow humans. American democracy is one of the greatest political espousals of such compassion. In the furor over religion and education, individuals of different ideological groups have come to forget compassion and instead hate those that they most want to convince. Democracy says that all of us can find standards of love, decency, respect, honesty, and responsibility—not by appealing to one's own version of beliefs but by allowing the religious or nonreligious beliefs of each to shine through and upon us all. As humans we can rule ourselves. I know what I speak of is utopian; but so are all religions utopian, and democracy is utopian. Wouldn't it be a much better world if we could be quiet, turn around, and listen to all of us seek heaven on earth?

━<small>◠◠◠</small>━ Who Owns the Child?

Ly wife, Sara, and I occasionally would remind our children, when they were trying to extend an evening curfew or were ignoring an order to clean their rooms, that we were their "owners" and that they could not do whatever they wished. We further explained that upon turning twenty-one, they would own themselves, and only then was individual liberty to be their prerogative. Although we said the words *owners* in good humor (at least we thought we were being humorous), there was seriousness behind the teasing words. Our daughters were—at the ages of twelve, fifteen, even twenty—our dependents. We, as parents, provided them with a home, food, and an allowance for their school, clothing, and transportation expenses. They also had the bonuses of our love and counsel, and we had the parental obligation to worry about them. After all, they were still children and were expected to comply with the small demands we made.

Years later, in a policy meeting with other educators deciding the best ways to dispense large sums of money for educational change, I argued that we needed to direct monies only to those public schools that had made a clear commitment to democratic learning and an effort to implement it to prepare students to become productive citizens of a democracy. A rural educator from Alabama, whom I respected greatly, looked at me incredulously and said, "you are absolutely wrong!" Having admired this person's work with students and high school faculties in developing educational programs with rural resources, I was stunned by this adamant rebuff to my position. I said, "Jack, what do you mean I am wrong? Preparing students to become citizens is the essence of your own work." "No," he replied, "We don't prepare them to be citizens—they *are* citizens! What they *do* with their citizenship is our work."

After the meeting, I consulted several legal experts and asked them if Jack was right, if students were citizens. He was and they are. All children born in the United States have, at birth, the full rights of American citizenship, and all naturalized minors have the same rights. In addition, they have other rights that give them added protections from adults. The only rights they don't have are the vote and other rights bestowed at prescribed ages (the rights to drive a car, to marry, to drink alcohol, and so on), generally between sixteen and twenty-one. This discovery (which, of course, I should have known) meant that I and Sara were incorrect in telling our children that we owned them—we didn't. But we certainly had an obligation as parents to provide for them, to guide them, and to expect them to be responsible. But the discussion with Jack raised, for me, the question of who does own children and therefore has the right and responsibility to educate them.

HOME VERSUS STATE SCHOOLING

This issue about responsibility for children and their education has been part of a lively correspondence between myself and a number of home-schooling parents. The home-school parents say that public or private schools should not educate or have any direct influence on the education of their children. In much of their arguments, they cite John Stuart Mill to defend the position that the education of children is the right of parents and not the state. Mill wrote, "A general state education is a mere contrivance for molding people to be exactly like one another; and as the mold in which it cases them is that which pleases the predominate power in the government, whether this be a monarch, a priesthood, an aristocracy, or the majority of the existing generation; in proportion as it is efficient and successful, it establishes a despotism over the mind, leading by natural tendency to one over the body" (quoted in Massaro, 1993, pp. 60–61).

These are strong words about the danger of state control over education. I concur that public schools, as state agents, can create "a despotism over the mind." However, the home-school parents omit in their correspondence that Mill also believed that parents *must* provide an appropriate education for their children, and if this is not done, then the parents must be subject to state punishment (Massaro, 1993, p. 60).

John Locke similarly argued that parents (that is, fathers) should use their parental desire and adult powers over their children to educate them well. Yet, Locke believed that such powers should not be unlimited or go unchecked. Exclusive authority on the part of parents does not guarantee liberty and freedom for every young citizen; likewise, exclusive authority on the part of the state does not ensure liberty and freedom. Absolute control by either parents or the state over children can create slavery (Gutmann, 1987, pp. 30–31). In a democracy, every child must be able to make up his or her own mind, free from all forms of tyranny over the mind, whether by the state, the community, or the family. Virtue in a democracy is acquired when every person has "the ability to deliberate among competing conceptions of the good" and form his or her own conclusions.

WHO SHOULD CONTROL EDUCATION?

So, to avoid tyranny, control over public education must be balanced. As Amy Gutmann wrote, "Because children are members of both families and states . . . the children are no more the property of their parents than they are the property of the state" (1987, p. 33).

As I have discussed with home-schooling advocates, neither the state nor the family is to be totally trusted. Home education, private education, and religious education all have the right to exist in a society that respects diversity, pluralism, and free association among individuals. Yet, home-schooling activities cannot be left totally alone; they must be monitored by the state to ensure that education is being provided and that parents, families, or communities do not violate the rights of a child.

[Education is essentially a state responsibility and thus requires state action.] A democratic society has the obligation to protect its children from laxness, abuse, and totalitarian thought. At the same time, it is every parent's obligation to ensure that public education and state schools are not a despotism of state control over the minds of children, and they have the right to change, alter, or dismantle public schools that mentally or physically harm students. Unchecked state or federal mandates that prescribe specific curricula, programs, and assessment instruments without the involvement of parents is tyranny, and unchecked parental mandates that prescribe how curricula, programs, and assessments are to work for their child are also tyranny. Any policies or mandates void of the local deliberations and checks and balances of state agents (that is, educators) against local parents and citizens are to be feared. Policies derived from a spectrum of educators, parents, and community members must never destroy democracy but must be a reasonable way to achieve the aspirations, principles, and laws of a democratic society. As Gutmann states, "A democratic theory of education recognizes the importance of empowering citizens to make educational policy. . . . But such policy must preserve the intellectual and social foundations of democratic deliberations" (1987, p. 14).

—᷈— Constitutional Hope for Education

Massaro wrote that "our national constitutional tradition is one of perpetual struggle to balance multiple competing concerns. . . . Americans are joined most distinctively and paradoxically by a constitutional commitment to the right to dissent. . . . The challenge . . . is to convey this struggle and paradox in terms that will enable all students to participate equally, meaningfully, and productively in it" (1993, p. 127).

The courts have generally ruled that decisions about curricula, pedagogy, teacher materials, and funding are decisions for local schools, districts, and states to make. When the courts do rule, they generally rule in the negative, telling schools what they must not do but not telling them what to do. (The most notable exceptions to this negative rule have been rulings in regard to inequitable financing of schools, such as in *Rose* v. *Council for Better Education* [1989]). Thus, most educators, parents, students, and school board members can be assured that as long as their decisions are based on valid educational considerations and do not impinge on protected rights, the courts will uphold those decisions against legal challenges. It is only when decisions are arbitrary or discriminatory or violate protected rights that the courts will find merit in a legal challenge to them.

This means that within those parameters, schools, school districts, and states have wide discretion over what goes into curricula, can circumscribe student expression, can select and remove books from classrooms and school libraries, can determine tests and requirements for all students, and can tell teachers what they can or cannot teach in regard to controversial issues. The reason that schools, districts, school boards, and state departments of education have great flexibility in such matters is to limit national control (spurred by ideological or political bias) over what can be thought and practiced. "What is clear is that the current court has left the matter almost entirely in the official's and citizen's hands" (Massaro, 1993, p. 104).

So although the court sees a clear democratic purpose in public schools, "the Constitution presupposes the existence of an informed citizenry prepared to participate in governmental affairs, and these democratic principles obviously are constitutionally incorporated into the structure of our government. It, therefore, seems entirely appropriate that the State use public schools to . . . inculcate fundamental values necessary to the maintenance of a democratic political system" (*Board of Education* v. *Pico*, 1982, p. 876).

The courts are intentionally vague in defining how public schools should go about teaching responsibilities of civility, values, public welfare, and democracy: "The process of educating youth for citizenship in public schools is not confined to books, the curriculum, and the civics class; schools must teach by example the shared values of a civilized social order. Consciously or otherwise, teachers—and indeed the older students—demonstrate the appropriate form of civil discourse and political expression by their conduct and deportment in and out of class (*Bethel School District* v. *Fraser,* 1986, p. 682).

Being specific would constrain freedom of dissent, but the courts do make clear the intended common responsibilities of schools. Schools are not to be used for sectarian, repressive, discriminating, and nondemocratic purposes; they are to educate for democratic purposes (Dayton & Glickman, 1994; Dayton, 1995).

So how to educate for democratic purposes is left mostly in the hands of local citizens, who determine what should be the values and practices of a nonrepressive and inclusive educational institution that must consider ideas and determine actions that have educational benefits for all. I believe that it is the failure to understand this responsibility that, at times, results in the lack of deliberations, repression and exclusion of contrary voices, and noneducative actions of schools. Allow me to state this another way. There is no one set of absolutely correct teaching and learning practices to achieve democratic purposes, but there is one essential element: the right of everyone to be involved fairly and justly in considering democratic ends for all students. No specific pedagogical method, activity, or curriculum can be justified as a clear constitutional right enforceable by law. Instead, what I speak of is a constitutional hope that the people, when informed, can determine their actions based on educational and democratic merit. As Massaro wrote, "the commitments set down in the Constitution are believed to have specific pedagogical implications. They imply a preference for methods of instruction that inspire critical deliberation, are tolerant of diverse viewpoints, and respect individual autonomy" (1993, p. 70).

The hope is that exchanges among diverse individuals will protect free thought for all citizens, further democratic ends, and encourage practices that accord the same respect for students and teachers. Democracy does not subscribe to any one individual's or group's idea of absolute truth. Absolute truth silences and controls the minds of citizens and suppresses freedom of expression and critical deliberation. The notion of absolute truth, often invoked in God's name, has been the most dangerous cause of exploitation and inhumanity toward other people. Education is the counterforce to such oppression. The governor of colonial Virginia, Sir William Berkeley, knew of the power of education to counter notions of absolute truth quite well when he wrote in 1671, "I thank God, there are no free schools. . . . Learning has brought disobedience . . . into the world" (quoted in Watson & Barber, 1988, p. 181).

Government control over citizens' thoughts—whether by a secular or a religious government—leads to the claim that absolute truth is known only by government leaders. We have enough evidence of what such control does—Hitler's Germany, the Crusades, the Vietnam War, Stalin's Russia, Mao's Red China, and now Nigeria, Bosnia, and Rwanda.

Those who fear that the public schools might become peddlers of "absolute truths" in a bid for state control over citizens' political thought have a very legitimate concern. Public schools should never teach one "correct" view—except the view that there is none. Those who argue that schools should teach absolute truths about morality, civility, and responsibility are misguided. Concern about lax morality, civility, and responsibility would be gone if schools understood that the only absolute value is democracy. The school's only responsibility to teach absolutes *is* to inculcate the values of democracy:

- All citizens are equal.
- All are entitled to life, liberty, and the pursuit of happiness.
- All are responsible for protecting freedom and justice, for themselves and for one another.
- Decisions are to be made of, by, and for the people, while always respecting the rights of the minority.

As Jefferson said, "nothing is unchangeable but the inherent and unalienable rights of man" (quoted in Arendt, 1963, p. 231).

For a democracy to thrive, it must always be open to exploring new ideas. Decisions must always be seen as temporary resting points based on the current wisdom of the people. If the people's decisions and actions do not create better individuals, communities, and governments, then the society needs to create more openness, exploration, and participation. In sum, it is the Jeffersonian belief in education and the people that safeguards decency and civility: "I know of no safe depository of the ultimate power of the society but the people themselves, and if we think them not enlightened enough to exercise their control with a wholesome discretion, the remedy is not to take it from them, but to inform their discretion" (quoted in Watson & Barber, 1988, p. 53).

Perhaps some specific issues will demonstrate the distinction between not teaching absolute truths and respecting absolute values.

1. *Not teaching an absolute truth.* Schools should censor reading materials for students and remove books that contain profanity or explicit sexual references.

   Respecting an absolute value. Such a decision to restrict or allow materials of interest to students should be decided by a democratic process that includes representatives of all citizens of the school community (older students, parents, community members, and educators). The decision should address the protection of free expression, the public welfare, academic freedom, the overall educational benefits of the materials, and the protection of justice and equality for all students.

2. *Not teaching an absolute truth.* Homosexuality should be taught as an acceptable lifestyle.

   Respecting an absolute value. All citizens, regardless of their sexual preference, are equal and are entitled to the same rights and have the same responsibilities as anyone else. Schools should not teach that any one lifestyle—heterosexual, homosexual, or bisexual—is "correct."

3. *Not teaching an absolute truth.* Creationism is absolutely wrong and should never be taught in public schools.

   Respecting an absolute value. Religious conceptions of how life began should be taught in schools as alternatives to scientific findings and theories. Religious concepts should not be taught *as* science, however, nor should schools advocate religious beliefs as "correct" beliefs.

4. *Not teaching an absolute truth.* Students should do what they are told without questioning authority.

   Respecting an absolute value. Students, as citizens, should learn to question, to pursue the truth, to speak freely, and to make up their own minds. At the same time, they need to learn to be respectful and considerate of those with greater wisdom and experience than their own. Students need to learn to express themselves in ways that do not infringe upon the rights of teachers to teach and other students to learn. Always there must be opportunities for students to ask questions and receive answers.

5. *Not teaching an absolute truth.* Students should be classified, labeled, and placed into groups, ranging from special education to gifted, so that individual abilities are recognized as fixed and stable.

   Respecting an absolute value. Placement decisions should be made on the following democratic criteria: (1) all students are equal; (2) every student is entitled to an education that will provide him or her full access to life, liberty, and the pursuit of happiness; and (3) justice and equality are essential for all. A school should make placement decisions using a process that involves the school community, based on a review of research on student learning in different types of placements. A decision about placement of students must be justified according to the democratic criteria of being nonrepressive and nondiscriminatory.

In general, if schools, communities, school boards, and states took seriously Madison's fourth proposal, which became the essence of the Bill of Rights, constitutional hope would become the everyday educational practices of our schools.

Madison wrote, "The Civil Rights of none shall be abridged on account of religious beliefs or worship, nor shall any national religion be established, nor shall the full and equal rights of conscience be in any manner, or on any pretext, infringed.

"The people shall not be deprived or abridged of their right to speak, to write or to publish their sentiments; and the freedom of the press, as one of the great bulwarks of liberty, shall be inviolable.

"The people shall not be restrained from peaceably assembling and consulting for their common good" (from the *Annals of Congress,* June 8, 1789; quoted in Peck, 1992, p. 71).

If these absolute values were followed, decisions of the school community would promote education as the common, democratic good.

PART FOUR

On Differences

Discussions about democracy as education are vaporous if we ignore the issue of equality and justice. Race, gender, ethnicity, socioeconomic status, and family background all contribute to who we are as individuals. In these essays I attempt to speak directly—and at times personally—to differences that have included some and excluded others from participating fully in classrooms, schools, education, and community life in America. My end point is that we should all be equal in the eyes of a practicing democracy. The family table of schools, communities, and society belongs to all of us—no one needs to be invited. In helping young people to excel at the American table, we need to understand and teach them as individuals of different cultures, backgrounds, and experiences.

~~~ Race and Education

"This group is too white and too right!" scolded a Texas state school board member in her closing comments to a three-day gathering of distinguished educational reformers and policymakers from throughout the United States. The group had convened in San Antonio to present, discuss, and develop policies for the next decade. The participants were sincere in speaking about the needs, challenges, and opportunities in reforming schools, refinancing public schools, changing governance structures, recruiting new teachers, and altering teacher education and leadership programs. What the Texas board member (a white female) wanted to make clear to all was that many people and other perspectives were absent. In the group of fifty-six invitees, there were only a few African Americans and Hispanic Americans and no Native Americans or Asian Americans. The formal papers were presented by white men and women, none with direct experience in the public schools. The irony of this is that the major point of agreement throughout the conference was the need for policies to "empower" educators and to "transform" and "decentralize" education. Now, I wish that I could report that this type of gathering was an exception to the major policy discussions that occur every day at the national, state, and district levels, but it was not. Even in reform efforts involving schools with large minority populations, major decisions about priorities, goals, and strategies are often made by leaders who do not represent those involved in the grassroots implementation. This is not solely a racial matter (which I will explain at another time), but it is a most glaring problem.

The reason that I begin this essay in this manner is to point out that even among what appear to be the most empathetic and educated white persons—people who wish to see a respectful, multicultural society at large—there is a lack of awareness of forming a multicultural society within their own sphere of control. In forming our network of schools in the mid-1980s, I was told by a black female principal of one of our pioneer schools that she didn't see a lot of people of color on the governing group, and we needed to do something about this (Glickman & Mells, 1997)! In essence, she was making the same point as Cornell West: it is the failure of many (whether liberal or conservative) to see that the participation of people of color "are neither additions to nor defections from American life, but rather *constitutive elements of that life*" (1993, p. 6).

As I move further into this essay, I admit of some trepidation. I can easily see some reader thinking that he's about to read the tired, knee-jerk liberal response of bending over backward to minorities. ("Why should a minority person be in a policy group? It should be merit, not race.") Or some other reader might think that this is going to be a paternalistic defense of insidious racism. ("Who is he, a white man, to write about and give ideas about people of color?") I'm sure that my own confusions about race and education will become apparent, and I'll need to check my tendency to give long explanations for each point that I make. To speak candidly of racial issues is not an easy task. In both public and private meetings, I have been accused by different people (both white and of color) of "selling out," "being a racist," and "doing what's right" in response to the same action. Any person, of whatever race, who has dealt with issues of race (rezoning schools, busing, financing, multicultural curricula, hiring and firing, and so on) has had similar experiences. Such charges have to be listened to seriously and acted upon or defended—and then one moves on. Even with excruciating concern over one's language usage, sensitivity to interpersonal relationships between people, and thoughtful development of ideas, polemic accusations, from whatever quarter, simply come with the territory of racial divisiveness in America. It is not my desire to avoid such charged encounters (even though I'd prefer them to be less charged) but instead to figure out how we the people, in all our "constitutive elements," can get beyond the charges and countercharges and deal with how to educate all our children well.

I am white—I guess. This is not how I identify myself, but in a society that labels its people into absolutes of white or nonwhite, I would have to check the white category.[1] I've spent a considerable amount of my time teaching in, attending, or otherwise participating in exclusively nonwhite schools and institutions. This in itself surprises some people. I believe that I received my first professional job due to assumptions by the hiring committee that I was African American, due to my having a graduate degree from a historically African American university. My grandparents came from Poland around 1910 as teenagers fleeing the Czar's army. My immediate ancestors had nothing to do with the slave trade, the exploitation of and cruelty to African Americans, the conscription of Chinese Americans to labor on U.S. railroads, the internment camps for Japanese Americans, the attempted eradication of Native Americans, or the subjugation of Mexican Americans. They were too busy trying to escape their own oppressors. However, I know that the crimes and the glories of America are my crimes and glories as well (Countryman, 1996; Lipset, 1996). In the academic lexicon, I know that I have been "privileged" by being perceived as white. I could and can move freely and inconspicuously (even though my parents couldn't) in the accepted channels, speaking the dominant language and adopting the manners of the dominant white society. When it came to "us versus them," I was and am one of the "us." No one needed to be overly concerned about how I would "fit in" among white colleagues or business acquaintances. So, I'm clear that my whiteness has given me an advantage over others. When I travel, I can walk into any major hotel appearing unshaved, wearing an old flannel shirt and worn blue jeans, and whether I'm staying there or not, I will not attract notice. I can take walks alone through any nicely manicured suburb in America and not be regarded with suspicion. I can drive over the speed limit in cities and counties and not worry that I might be pulled over and interrogated for far more than a traffic violation. (In today's newspaper, I just read that a senior vice president, wearing a three-piece suit and carrying an expensive leather briefcase, was pulled out of a commuter train in New

York State and frisked by police simply because they were looking for a black suspect, and he was the only black person in the train car. His appearance bore no resemblance—in terms of his figure, height, or weight—to the suspect the police were looking for. Only his skin color matched [Genasci, 1995a].) So my lack of duplicity in the sins of oppression in America do not get me off the hook. Racism has worked to my advantage, and if it is left unchecked, it will continue to privilege me and my own children in terms of access to education, careers, and wealth, and will continue to disadvantage others.

MY CONFUSIONS

I live in Georgia, and when northern friends ask me about race relations in the South, I say that they are wonderful and they are terrible (Betts, 1996). In Atlanta, in corporate life, in government, and in academia, there is a great casual flow among African Americans and whites. One will see people of all races working together, eating lunch together, socializing, living together, and marrying. I believe that Atlanta is much further ahead in race relations than most cities, and I wish more people from my northern homeland could see the reality of what America could someday be like. Yet, is what I see really true? Only at one level is it so. It is at the level of highly educated, successful, and upwardly aspiring people of all races. They have more in common, in terms of education and financial status, than there are differences among them. Yet, among individuals of lower socioeconomic status, Atlanta presents a totally different picture, of blatant isolation and discrimination. The apartheid of the former South Africa is closer to the picture of reality in Atlanta than some multicultural utopia. Many of Atlanta's inner-city communities (inside Interstate 285) are composed of a high concentration of people who are poor, and they are entirely African American. Crime, drugs, welfare, teenage pregnancies, and overall neglect are alarmingly high. The race picture is equally confused throughout the state, in rural and suburban lands, where there are notably well integrated areas as well as areas that are still bastions of the Old South. Similar situations can be seen among other racial or ethnic groups in northern New England (French, Native Americans, Anglos), the West (Asians, Hispanics, African Americans, Anglos), Hawaii (the rice people and the potato people), Alaska (the Tlingits, the Intuit, the Haidas, the Athabascans, Anglos), and so on.

The same contrasts are evident in schools in different communities across the nation. Minority students have made significant gains in narrowing the educational gaps between themselves and their white counterparts in the past decade (as measured by achievement scores, high school completion rates, rates of college acceptance), and there is now a very significant minority middle class (Jennings, 1996). For example, 40 percent of African Americans are solidly in the middle class (a jump from 5 percent before 1960), and unprecedented numbers of Asian and Hispanic Americans have attained advanced degrees and successful careers ("Hispanic-Owned Firms Outpace Business Expansion," 1996).

So on the one hand it becomes hard to sympathize with minorities, of whatever race or culture, who have acquired great wealth and influence yet still claim to be victims of discrimination. Others—minorities or not—would like to be so victimized! Yet from those members of minority groups who remain in poverty without much, if any, hope—and their numbers continue to grow—the cries of victimization are increasingly poignant and urgent (Hacker, 1992). It's unclear to me, looking at the two cases—one of success and the other of despair—how to know whether the issue of discrimination and oppression is mostly a matter of race or also to an important extent a matter of class. In polls of minorities, members of lower socioeconomic classes think that middle- and upper-class members of their own racial group do not understand or empathize with their situation, just as whites don't. This is perhaps what is meant when one member of a minority group refers to another member as "not really being one of us." What is implied is that the other person, because of their success in the larger society, doesn't understand the language, culture, or lifestyle of those who remain in poverty and "with" their own minority group.

My last confusion is over integration. What at one time appeared to be a reasonable strategy for attaining an integrated society at a later time appears to be foolish at best or counterproductive at worst. Let me explain. Integrating schools was seen by the U.S. Supreme Court and later by the federal officials who wrote the desegregation guidelines as a way to promote equality in education, greater economic opportunity for minorities, and an integrated society overall. In 1968, at age twenty-one, I became a federally sponsored teacher corps intern assisting in the integration of schools in an isolated rural community in the Chesapeake Bay area of Virginia. The first year, I was one of three white teachers in an entirely African American school. The second year, I taught in the first consolidated and integrated school. At the time of integration, the schools were composed of approximately two-thirds white and one-third black students. The idea behind integration was that by having black and white students attend the same schools, they would learn from one another, educational achievement would improve among minority children, and the patterns of social and economic isolation and discrimination by race would be eliminated.

In 1995, twenty-seven years later, my wife and I returned to the same Chesapeake Bay town for a short visit. When asking about former black students and their families, we found that most had moved away a long time ago to the nearest metropolitan city, about fifty miles away. Upon visiting our former school, my wife and I, to our utter surprise, saw only a few black children in a sea of white children on the playgrounds. Later in the day we again saw mainly white children walking home or boarding the school buses. Upon asking a teacher friend who still lived in the area, we were told that the black population was now less than 5 percent in the county and was continuing to decline. So what had actually happened over the span of three decades was the opposite of what the plan to achieve racial integration had intended (Orfield, 1993). African Americans who attended segregated schools in the era before the civil rights movement have offered some tentative suggestions, based on their experience, to explain what happened (see Delpit, 1994; Irvine, 1990, Irvine & Foster, 1996). The African American school had in many ways been one of the institutional anchors of black community life. When it ended and the new era of integration began, this institutional anchor of care, concern, support, and involvement for black children was lost. The result was a movement by blacks—no doubt accelerated by continuing poverty and a lack of economic opportunities in integrated areas—to relocate to the more racially isolated communities found in metropolitan areas (Lemann, 1995a). What is remarkable about this is that before school integration, there was greater geographic integration of the races in this rural community. Blacks and whites used to live across the road or next to each other. So, the dramatic Supreme Court and federal actions to break the isolation of the races through education actually resulted in their greater isolation from one another. So who, in the end, gained? This sobering story of discontinuity and reverse effects has been told to me over and over again, not only in rural but in urban areas as well. Such stories are laced with the sadness of African Americans at the closing of black schools and their confusion over the need for integrated ones (Hunter-Gault, 1992).

Diane Ravitch has puzzled about whether the strategy of integration, which aimed to equalize education by having black students become a minority population within predominantly white schools, was the result of white society's inability to imagine that a minority school could be a good school. If so, such thinking "could not extricate itself from the very racism that it so passionately denounced" (1983, p. 173). And as Gutmann wrote, "Studies show that desegregation in its minimal form—busing black and/or white students to achieve 'racial balance' but making no substantial changes in the way students are educated within schools—may augment racial prejudice and decrease the educational achievement of black students" (1987, p. 164).

WHAT IS EDUCATIONAL RACISM?

Since *racism* is a word used often in any heated discussion between people of different races, I think that we need to explore the word carefully and make specific distinctions between what is and isn't racism in education and schools. Racism is "a program or practice of racial discrimination, segregation, persecution, and domination, based on racialism, a doctrine or feeling of racial . . . antagonisms especially with reference to supposed racial superiority, inferiority, or purity" (Guralnik & Friend, 1962, p. 1198).

For example, it is difficult for many people to believe that when one person argues against their point of view about matters of race or class that the contrary opinion isn't "racist" or "classist." For example, liberals often believe that if conservatives don't agree with them on social issues such as welfare or crime, then the conservatives are being racist. At times, parents of one race believe that if their child is being disciplined by a teacher of another race, then the teacher is racist. It rarely occurs to people who freely throw around the charge of racism that race may not be a factor in other people's disagreeing with them on a given issue. Of course, there are times when people do espouse ideas or act in ways that overtly or covertly show them to be racist. But just because someone disagrees or acts less than harmoniously with another doesn't automatically mean that the person is a bigot. (I know that some readers may be chafing at these statements, but please hear me out.)

Take the realm of contemporary politics as an example. I believe that Newt Gingrich is not a racist. Although I may disagree strongly with what he recommends in regard to privatization, welfare, education, and affirmative action, I find nothing in his manner, his language, and his reasoning that suggests to me that he believes that any person in America is inferior to another due to race or that he is any less committed to a fully integrated society than any other citizen. What Gingrich proposes to do about these issues will, in my opinion, aggravate rather than solve racial and class divisions, but he does not believe that to be so. As two people we simply, and strongly, disagree with each other. On the other hand, there are others who advocate similar plans concerning privatization, welfare, vouchers, and education who clearly do so with racist intent. In private conversations with some of these advocates, it is obvious that class privilege and race separations are what they wish to preserve. For example, a white woman advocating privatization of education took issue with my public stance against using vouchers to support private schools. She candidly confided in me, "I want you to know I'm against race mixing, and I support vouchers because they would allow the races to stay apart. Don't get me wrong; I'm not a racist." Despite this person's public pronouncements about academic excellence and the need for competition between public and private schools, she was and is a racist. My point is that there are some who argue for school choice, vouchers, and grouping (tracking) of students not because they are prejudiced but because they simply believe that such policies represent the best way to educate students and that every child, regardless of his or her race, gender, or class, should be challenged by working with a similar academic peer group.

An Asian teacher who suspends a white child for throwing a book at her is not automatically a racist. A school that has more severe discipline problems with students from a particular race, culture, or socioeconomic group and thus takes more corrective actions against them is not automatically racist or classist. Such incidents certainly raise the issue of why a teacher has more problems with a particular student or why a school has disproportionate problems with large numbers of students of a certain group, but again, the reason may not always be unfair or discriminatory treatment. It may be that in some classrooms or schools, some students of some groups simply break more rules than others. It may be that these students do not understand or respect the rules. It may be that in their own home, community, or peer group there are different norms of behavior. It may be that a teacher unknowingly acts in ways that annoy or frustrate them. Or perhaps the teacher and school have not developed educational practices and programs sensitive to the needs, aspirations, and learning styles of children who are members of a particular group or groups. All of these are reasonable possibilities that fall quite short of racism. Racism may be the reason for how certain students are treated in a school. I certainly don't deny that it exists. (And it is often easier to detect among members of the same racial group than publicly, within integrated groups.) But my disclaimer is that racism is not always the explanation when a member of one racial group doesn't like a member of another group.

TIME TO RETURN HOME—
DEMOCRACY AS EDUCATION

For a time, there was a popular slogan on T-shirts worn by African American youths: "It's a black thing. You wouldn't understand." I'm sure that such a statement captures the sentiments of other racial, cultural, gender, or economic groups. "It's a Native American (or Asian, Hispanic, Italian, Jewish, Serbian) thing. You wouldn't understand." I believe such statements are correct; I cannot understand the history, customs, culture, and perspectives of other people as well as I understand my own. If I'm not poor, it's hard for me to understand the perspective of poor people. Likewise, if I'm not a woman (or an Irish American, and so on), I cannot understand as fully as they can their own lives. My own experiences as a member of a historically persecuted group do not equate with the discrimination experienced by members of other groups. Yet, I only can come closer to understanding someone else if we acknowledge that we can never truly understand each other, but still attempt to do so. It's in the acknowledgment and the attempt that a public is gained, and public actions can be pursued. We can try. We always will fall short, so we will have to keep trying. The impossibility of complete understanding and agreement is the eternal challenge and value of democracy. As Cornell West wrote, "Since democracy is, as the great Reinhold Niebuhr noted, a proximate solution to insoluble problems, I envision neither a social utopia nor a political paradise." But, he continued, "We simply cannot enter the twenty-first century at each other's throats, even as we acknowledge the weighty forces of racism, patriarchy, economic inequality, homophobia, and ecological abuse on our necks" (1993, p. 159). So when it comes to the issue of educating the next generation of citizens, rather than walking past each other in silence or shouting prejudiced charges, might we try the proximate solution?

Note

1. A push by multiracial Americans to add another classification, "multiracial," to the U.S. census may signal a major, positive change in how we think of Americans (see "Rally Held for Multiracial Category on 2000 Census," 1996).

Suffrage, Gender, and Listening

In 1853, Sojourner Truth spoke at the Fourth National Woman's Rights Convention: "I know that it feels a kind o' hissin' and ticklin' like to see a coloured woman get up and tell you about things, and woman's rights. We have all been thrown down so low that no body thought we'd ever get up again but . . . we will come up again and . . . we'll have our rights. . . . You may hiss as much as you like, but it is coming" (quoted in Zinn, 1980, p. 180).

Jane Addams, Grace and Edith Abbott, Alice Hamilton, Julia Lathrop, and Florence Kelly made great progress in promoting social reform and forging labor agreements and child protection laws. The tireless work of Susan B. Anthony and others resulted in the passage in 1920 of the Nineteenth Amendment, conferring upon women the vote. During the first two decades of the twentieth century, Ella Flagg Young and Margaret Haley took major roles in education—Young as the superintendent of schools in Chicago and Haley as president of the country's major teachers' association. Young was so optimistic about the initial successes of pioneer women in education that, in 1909, she wrote, "Women are destined to rule the schools of every city. . . . In the near future we shall have more women than men in executive charge of the vast educational system" (quoted in Tyack & Cuban, 1995, p. 265).

Yet more than seventy years later, women still remain removed from most of the leadership roles in schools, communities, businesses, and government. (Nearly 90 percent of all federal legislators are male; America ranks forty-third of all countries in terms of women in its national legislature ["World's Women Still Have Far to Go," 1995; Cook, 1996]). Linquist Deborah Tannen writes about how American politics has retained the masculine perspective of the nineteenth century: "It's still so clear that it was structured with a male audience in mind. . . . There's all the sports analogies, the ritual opposition, the warlike debate formats, even the ways our leaders get points for being successful in military situations" (quoted in Stark, 1996, p. 74).

Having the vote is not the same thing as having the ability to influence important decisions. To vote is to choose between given alternatives, to participate is to help determine the alternatives that are offered. As Helen Keller lamented, "Our democracy is but a name. We vote. What does that mean? It means that we choose . . . between Tweedledum and Tweedledee" (Zinn, 1980, p. 337).

Sue Middleton wrote that women have been taught in schools, in businesses, and in neighborhoods that their ideas are less important than men's. Upon accepting an appointment as an academician, she still doubted her competence, because others had led her to believe that a woman could really have nothing important to say: "Like many women academics I felt shaky, insecure in my role as an expert, disbelieving in my right to teach and my authority" (1993, p. 112).

A female high school teacher and former graduate student of mine explained why she so often declined to speak at her school faculty meetings: "All my adult life, I've felt like a pretender—pretending to be smart, pretending to be articulate, pretending to have original ideas. I keep thinking that if I speak out, they will uncover me for what they already think I am—just another 'too smart for her own good woman.'"

What is known as the "second wave" of the women's movement in America, occurring in the late twentieth century, gained momentum when women shared with one another common stories and frustrations about their expected roles (social, economic, intellectual, and sexual) in a male-dominated society. These insights came about from women talking together outside the company of men. Women found that discussions about issues of gender with men were difficult to hold, as men tended to monopolize the talk with what *they* thought about women's issues or how *they* reacted and responded to feminist issues. Many women felt limited and defensive discussing a subject with males that only they truly knew for themselves.

What is particularly revealing is that the second wave of the women's consciousness movement arose from the experience of many female participants involved in the human rights and other social protest movements of the 1960s. Women participating in these movements found themselves relegated to performing clerical tasks, cooking meals, and running errands. They were excluded from the planning meetings, held by men, ostensibly to decide how to gain greater equality and liberty for all. Male chauvinism was as prevalent among enlightened "liberal" men as among self-proclaimed conservatives. Thus, women found themselves having to liberate themselves from their supposed liberators. This could only be done by talking and sharing previously unspoken thoughts and feelings with other women.

When women held their own meetings, what happened, according to Ann Floreman, was that they learned "to look at themselves through their own eyes rather than through those of men . . . the . . . often painful process of breaking through the experiences of femininity. By discussing and comparing their individual experiences women developed an understanding of the emotional structures of their dependency" (quoted in Middleton, 1993, p. 113).

WHAT WOULD BE DIFFERENT WITH FULL PARTICIPATION?

In national elections, going back to George Wallace's campaign for president, hard-line, confrontational candidates who pit one group of people against another have received greater voter support from males than from females (Stark, 1996, p. 76). Although many media accounts still suggest that the gender gap is greatest on "women's issues" (abortion, family benefits, equal pay), the fact is that the gulf between women and men is wider on general domestic affairs issues (Stark, 1996, p. 72). For example, according to a 1990 poll by the League of Women Voters, the majority of women believe that balancing the budget should be done gradually and should not hurt people dependent on current programs. Similarly, most women believe that changing social welfare programs should include increased attention to child care and job training and that state and federal government should play a more active social role in countering discrimination and helping families (Cook, 1996). Thus, if women had an equal influence on societal decisions rather than merely an equal vote, current perspectives on government policy would be different. More attention would be paid to caring for people (Noddings, 1992), and there would be less equating of educational success with "whether the child has maintained or suppressed the socio-economic status of [his or her] parents" (Grumet, quoted in Middleton, 1993, p. 56). Furthermore, in my opinion, students would be educated better and be part of a more just, equal, and civil society if women were full partners in all aspects of education and society.

How can such equality be realized in a society where men are still firmly in control of the vast apparatus of politics, government, business, education, and other international and domestic institutions? Cornell West (1996) explains that every American possesses prejudices and stereotypes, directed not only at those of a different gender, race, ethnicity, and so on but also at others within one's own group. The degree of prejudice may be more or less, depending on the individual, but it is still there.

So, let me acknowledge how I as a male often think about my own stereotypes and prejudices toward women and what I try to do to acknowledge, check, and act to promote greater democratic inclusiveness. I, and I think most other men (and women), do notice if a person I have just met is a woman or a man, tall or short, slight or large, colorfully or plainly robed, quiet or loud, and so on. I don't typically think of a person by a sole characteristic, but gender is one of the predominant traits by which I first identify another person. So when someone asks me to describe a new acquaintance, I generally start by stating that the person is a he or a she and then go on from there.

After I have observed and identified a person as male or female, the next question is how should I, as a man, respond to the person, if a female? I tend to be more relaxed when first meeting a woman than when first meeting a man. I do not see women initially as trying to find areas of competitive advantage. I stereotypically think that women are more apt to relate to another person as simply another person and not be overly concerned about the importance of job, status, or influence. My stereotypical thinking is that women tend to find common areas of discussion and are more willing to listen to others' ideas—at times with greater deference to a man's ideas than to their own. (As I read what I write, I know that these words are terribly simplistic and overgeneralized, but I'm trying to be candid). Now, as a male, I can use my thinking to my advantage, or I can acknowledge my thinking for what it is (stereotypical and simplistic), suspend it, and allow myself to try to understand the person as an individual rather than as a representative of a certain gender, race, culture, socioeconomic class, and so on.

If I take advantage of my gender and resort to a conditioned response concerning how a male is "supposed" to act in relation to a female, I would initiate the talk, monopolize the discussion, interrupt frequently, and press ahead with a "sticking to the point" discourse of the correctness of my ideas. If the female accepts my stereotype, she probably will listen patiently and at least pretend interest in my views. However, if she does not accept this stereotype, she will enter the discussion with equal or greater force, tell me to wait and not interrupt, and confront me to consider other ideas and other ways of handling situations that are based on criteria different from my own. If she refuses to accept the stereotype of female in relation to male and if I resist stereotypical responses, I will come to understand and learn from her in ways previously closed to me. (This discussion is from my, male, point of view, and I'm aware that even my choice of the words *allow* and *accept* indicates an orientation of control. Obviously, anyone who is an equal will not wait for someone else to extend an invitation; they will attend and participate of their own volition.)

Finally, who should control the agenda? Who should hold the floor, and who should listen to whom? Research has pointed out that control according to gender has been mostly one-sided—men control the agenda, more men hold the floor longer, and women listen to men more. In my own observations of classrooms, schools, and community group settings, I am very much aware of how disproportionately men initiate talk, interrupt, and hold the floor, and I know that active facilitation is necessary to rectify this imbalance. To do so, men need to concede more to women, until there are no distinguishable differences in the flow of discourse on issues and influence on the outcome of decisions. Thus I believe that women should have greater influence over the educational agenda, women should speak more frequently than men, and men should listen to women. This doesn't mean that men shouldn't speak, participate, or assert their views; it means that they should spend more time learning from the untapped experience, concerns, and knowledge of those who have been physically present in the past but often intellectually invisible.

SO HOW SHOULD WE EDUCATE IN REFERENCE TO GENDER?

It is limiting to education and to society to expect men to excel in certain endeavors but to expect less of women (see Evans, 1989). Classrooms and schools that give boys more room than girls to talk and be active; that direct boys more than girls toward science, math, and technology; and that provide more leadership roles for males restrict the potential of female students to excel (U.S. General Accounting Office, 1996, p. 5). To expect female students to excel more in the humanities and in "caring," "nurturing," "supportive" roles (and likewise counsel boys away from such interests and roles) also discriminates and restricts students' potential. We have enough individual examples to know that in adult life, men can be excellent nurturers, caretakers, and homemakers, and women can be excellent military leaders and corporate executives, and some can be both.

What someone chooses to do should not be the purpose of classrooms, schools, and democratic education. How a person experiences the world and how others perceive a person are not necessarily solely gender related but are multifaceted phenomena. Women and men will always be categorized by gender, but people as individuals are defined in many additional ways as well—by family and cultural background, education, socioeconomic status, race, occupation, religion, region, physical and personality attributes, and so on. The purpose should be to provide an education that equips individuals to have choices. Women's improved access to societal choices has been one of America's greatest achievements, but as a society we continue to lose when women's experiences and wisdom are not a full and equal part of classrooms, schools, and community and national leadership.

My first inclination in concluding this essay is to give examples of specific educational methods, activities, and organizations that aim to provide the same equal opportunities to females as males—ways to promote greater involvement of females in the life of classrooms, schools, and the larger community (American Association of University Women, 1992, 1996). I could list my opinions on the issue; but I'll check that inclination and instead listen to women—young and old—discuss what they have experienced as obstacles and possibilities and what they think should be done to provide a democratic education that is just and equal for all. I will be still, and I will listen. Perhaps, in time, I will be invited to be part of the discussion.

⟶ From Our Ancestors

The Native American writer Leslie Marman Silko, in her spellbinding book *Ceremony,* writes of the great alienation that results from trying to return to one's ancestors' culture while at the same time being pushed to assimilate into a modern society: "But he had known the answer all along, even while the white doctors were telling him he could get well and he was trying to believe them; medicine didn't work that way. Because the world didn't work that way. His sickness was only part of something larger, and his cure would be found only in something great and inclusive of everything" (1977, pp. 125–126).

The role of ceremony, if understood as changeable, can create a way to integrate both worlds: "She taught me this above all else: things which don't shift and grow are dead things. . . . That's what the witchery is counting on: that we will cling to the ceremonies the way they were, and then their power will triumph, and the people will be no more" (p. 126).

How does one look to the past in preserving the essence of ancestral life while still moving into a future of uncertainty and unpredictability with less familiar people and new points of view? How does anyone—from whatever racial, cultural, ethnic, religious, socioeconomic, or gender group—find the knowledge, understanding, and competence to take pride in their group's traditions and past and yet still be a fully valued and contributing member of future and larger communities? We can gain insight from great teachers and teaching cultures of both the past and the present. In this essay I examine the teachings of Socrates, Jesus of Nazareth, and Jean Piaget and explore the educational traditions of Jewish Americans, Native Americans, Hispanic Americans, African Americans, and Asian Americans.[1] In so doing I conclude that these teachers and cultures are not different in how they value learning—they all respect ceremony as it pertains to the individual student in present public life.

Let's begin with Socrates. Socrates would frustrate his friends with his unwillingness to teach and to give them answers. He said, "You must think I am most singularly fortunate my dear Meno to know whether virtue can be taught or how it is acquired. The fact is that far from knowing whether it can be taught, I have no idea what virtue itself is" (*Plato's Meno,* 71a, trans. 1976).

He then confuses Meno further by saying that not knowing is good, because it helps people pursue, rather than be told, answers. Thus Socrates' means of teaching was to ask questions to help students form their own answers: "We shall be better, braver, and more active . . . if we believe it right to look for what we don't know" (86c).

Four hundred years later, Jesus of Nazareth was raised in a teaching culture that stressed interpretation and discussion. At the age of twelve, Jesus separated himself from his family and went to study in the Temple of Jerusalem. He spent three days sitting with rabbinical teachers, "listening to them and asking them questions" (2 Luke 41:47, Standard Version). The nature of his learning experience is captured by Zborowski's observation of traditional Jewish teachings. Zborowski describes a typical lesson Jewish children learn from their religious teacher: "Almost every sentence [of the teacher] was challenged by the pupils. . . . Sometimes they attacked the teacher in groups . . . in a struggle which knew no bounds. At this time the great teacher sat calmly and quietly without saying a word, as if he were thinking, 'Go ahead, children, go ahead'" (Mead & Wolfenstein, 1955, p. 128).

This type of learning experience and way of pursuing truth in Jesus' culture helps explain why the adult Jesus rarely lectured to his followers (the most notable exception being the Sermon on the Mount). Mostly, he asked others to initiate their own learning: "Seek and ye shall find" (Matthew 7:7). He talked in parables so that others could discern their own meaning, and he chastised those who regarded religion as a set of laws to be slavishly followed: "Woe to you teachers of the law! For you have taken away the key of knowledge; you did not enter yourself, and you hindered those who were entering" (Luke 11:52).

We can see the same view of learning—of initiating, pursuing, and guiding—in the culture of the Native Americans. Norbert Hill wrote of the "Indian Way," "the universe is the 'university.' The acquisition of [learning] was largely a by-product of life experiences, including observation and participation in the activities of adults. . . . Assistance and guidance, rather than domination and control, were the way of our elders, our greatest teachers. . . . An enlightened teacher would encourage students to engage their curiosity through co-generating and participating in a variety of activities"
(1993, pp. 171–173).

In a similar manner, Sonia Nieto and Carmen Rólon summarize their studies of teaching practices for Hispanic students: "Providing for academic intimacy between students and teachers . . . small group discussions, learning partners, and heterogeneous groups . . . increasing students' active participation and leadership responsibilities inside and outside the classroom . . . student-selected topics for presentations . . . these strategies . . . are effective in improving the achievement of Latino students" (Nieto & Rólon, 1995, p. 22).

The African American educator Gloria Ladson-Billings, in her recent study of successful teachers of African American children, describes a public school that is responsive to the traditions of African American culture: "[the school] has one requirement—that its students be successful. The curriculum is rigorous and exciting. The student learning is organized around problems and issues. . . . The students have studied cities in ancient African Kingdoms, Europe, and Asia. They are studying their own city. They have taken trips to City Hall. . . . Groups of students are working on solutions to problems specific to the city" (1994, pp. 140–141).

And finally, the great European cognitive psychologist Jean Piaget summarized his lifetime of studying learning by saying that students come to learn most successfully in this way: "The active school . . . presupposes working in common, alternating between individual work and work in groups, since collective living has been shown to be essential to the full development of the personality in all its facets—even the more intellectual" (1974, pp. 108–109). He also said that "the goal of intellectual education is not to know how to repeat or retain ready-made truths (a truth that is parroted is only a half-truth). It is in learning to master the truth by oneself at the risk of losing a lot of time and of going through all the roundabout ways that are inherent in real activity" (p. 106).

What we can cull from these diverse teachers and cultures is that there is a common essence to the process of learning that transcends ethnicity, race, and culture. It is a pedagogy of democracy, a process that respects the student's own desire to know, to discuss, to solve problems, and to explore individually and with others, rather than to have learning dictated and determined by the teacher.

We have confused the concepts of teaching individuals *as* members of a particular culture or group versus teaching individuals *about* their cultural group (and others') so that they may better understand and appreciate it. Because some anthropologists claim that Native American children learn best through cooperative methods, it should not be assumed that this is the proper or best way in all situations to teach all Native American students. Because Asian American students are most popularly identified, according to Pang (1995), as diligent, quiet, and obedient achievers (the "model-minority myth"), it should not be assumed that all Asian students should be taught by authoritarian approaches. Because some researchers conclude that African American family culture is expressive and kinesthetic (Irvine, 1990), it should not be assumed that every individual student of African American ancestry will learn best in an expressive and kinesthetic environment. Because some scholars (Castañeda, 1995) conclude that Mexican American culture emphasizes the rhythmic nature of time rather than discrete time segments, it should not be assumed that each individual student who happens to be Mexican American would be best taught free of schedules. If historians note that European Americans come from a culture of linear and sequential thinking, this does not mean that every individual of European ancestry should be taught in a linear, sequential manner. Any generalizations about students drawn from supposed characteristics of a single cultural group can become stereotypes that force students into culturally identified modes of learning, whether appropriate for them or not. Is there something wrong with a student if he doesn't conform and respond willingly to such culturally specific strategies? Is he denying his heritage? No—it is as dangerous to force a particular cultural expectation upon an individual student as it is to refuse to use a student's culture in understanding appropriate ways of helping her learn.

A student is an individual first, before he or she is a member of a cultural group. There may be as many individual differences in learning, valuing, and seeing within a group as there are differences across cultures. It is imperative to know the *student* first—not the culture, not the family, not the neighborhood. By knowing the student well, one then learns the influence of his or her history, family, and community. It is through encouraging students to add their cultural influences to the learning of all the other students in their classroom that they can be allowed to "live" their history. In doing so, teachers and students respect and learn from one another as individuals of various histories, perspectives, and cultures.

An example might be illustrative of both the danger of cultural stereotyping and the advantage of building upon cultural influences. I am an Anglicized person—my language, manners, and appearance are in most ways indistinguishable from the group referred to as white Anglo-Saxon Protestants. Yet this group was not my total lived history. I was raised in a home with Jewish parents who, one generation removed, came from isolated, rural ghettos of Poland and Russia. My childhood was lived in at least three worlds: the Jewish world of the Ghetto (I remember Yiddish being spoken around me), the contemporary world of secularized Jewish people (my parents' generation was suburbanized and urbanized), and the Christian world that I encountered through television, trips outside of home, and fellow students in high school. All of these influences were part of my "lived" early history. For a school to educate me as if I had only one lived history—rural Jewish, secular immigrant, or assimilated— would have been unfair to me. For my teachers not to appreciate, understand, and build upon these histories and influences also would have been unfair. To educate me as if these three parts of my lived cultural history were my total past would have limited my learning with others. Instead, a democratic learning environment helped me find, appreciate, and express who I am—the product of a multitude of manifestations and influences (Cochran-Smith, 1995; Pang, 1994; Ladson-Billings, 1995).

The pedagogy of democracy has students work in settings, individually and collectively, that allow the experiences of all students (and teachers) to be resources for all. Thus students learn that the histories of their classmates' cultural groups are not the histories of "others" but their own history as well, the history of America (Cornbleth & Waugh, 1995, p. 198).

APPLICATIONS

What direct applications can be drawn from this? Let me attempt only a few for illustration purposes. A young student who does not speak English should not be taught solely in his native tongue, but his school should support his efforts to use his native language as he learns standard English. Allow him to explain, share, and teach his language and customs to others. Because a fifteen-year-old student comes from an oral culture with a lively tradition of storytelling, don't discourage (or expect) oral expressiveness, but encourage her to learn other forms of communication as well, including formal writing and speaking. We should build upon and support how students came to be who they are, but we should also challenge them to reach beyond. At the end, educators should always consider the individual first and the individual's ethnic, racial, or cultural group as critical but secondary information for understanding him or her. The purpose is to bring all individuals together into a larger, richer association of learning than if they remained tethered to the assumptions and expectations of one cultural group (Pang, 1994; Delpit, 1994).

In doing so, we provide an education that opens windows to new possibilities, recognizes in practice that democracies live through a common learning process that respects and builds upon differences among equals, gives to those students from groups who have been excluded in the past the same learning competence as students from groups who have been in control, and finally, allows the "ceremonies" of our ancestors to thrive in the present, because "we no longer cling to the way they were."

Note

1. I am indebted to the work of Corliss Harmer (1994).

PART FIVE

On Change

After reading the essays in the prior sections of this book, my colleagues (school practitioners, senior policymakers, and students) asked me to go further—to write essays on change, power, and activism. They felt that I was either ignoring or avoiding explaining my experiences with classroom and school change. I protested, saying that all my previous writings had been about such issues of leadership and change, and I wanted this book to focus on understanding democracy and education, the foundation for change. I believed that asking the right question about change—why educate and for what purpose—would lead to thoughtful answers from teachers, school leaders, parents, and other community members.

But my colleagues persisted. At a breakfast meeting, one of my senior colleagues, a renowned critic of past educational reform efforts, reiterated to me that what I had written so far "conveyed the impression that if all factions would only agree on what is 'public, democratic good,' the clouds would part and the sun of reason would dissolve the disagreements. But the warring factions see the world so differently that you have a responsibility to say what you would do in the real world of politics, religion, power, and contradictory ideologies."

So, after thinking over these points, I agreed to do so. The following essays are intended to deal with practical aspects of influence, change, and power. I begin by looking at activism, moving from the teacher and classroom level to the school and community level. I explain how I teach using student voice as a spur to my own changes as a classroom teacher. And finally, I address how to confront hierarchical control and use facilitation, resistance, and influence to move the educational system toward democracy, both as a means and an end. To my friend, thanks for the push.

Finding Room
for School Change

"For years, I believed that I was doing the best I could, that not all kids were cut out to do well . . . and that simply was the way it was" (Wasley, 1994, p. 75). Later, this same high school teacher, in consulting with others, was challenged to stop complaining that "my students just don't think" and start responding to the question, "Well, how do you give them a chance to?" Thus began a series of changes in this teacher's classroom practice.

Virginia Woolf (1978) wrote that a writer needs a private space for thinking and trying out ideas. It needs to be a protected space, so that the turmoil of starts and stops, elation and failures can be viewed as part of a journey of writing, of unfolding, discarding, and rewriting. A similar space is needed by teachers changing their classroom practice. It will be less private than a writer's space, as it will contain twenty to thirty students or more, and there will be parents, faculty, staff, and administrators with at least a casual interest in what is happening. The teacher's space must be at least psychologically protected, however, if not physically separated by a closed door or partition. The physical space can be more open if the teacher is supported by empathetic administrators and colleagues who convey the message, "It's okay to

137

change. We will listen, help, and keep others from being too quick to criticize." The optimal environment for change is a school and community in which norms of trust and intellectual challenge are part of the expectations of all participants, a place in which to change is to do one's work. As hooks points out, in such an environment "our purpose . . . is not to feel good. . . . Nor does it deny the reality that learning can be painful. And sometimes it's necessary to remind students and colleagues that pain and painful situations don't necessarily translate into harm. . . . Not all pain is harmful, and not all pleasure is good" (1995, p. 154).

Working toward a pedagogy of democracy—by listening to students and allowing for greater choice, activity, connections, contributions, and demonstrations of learning—will create pain and confusion among teachers, students, and colleagues. Some may perceive such changes as an abandonment of the traditional authority and secure routines of classrooms and schools that have defined the most prevalent practice of public education (McNeil, 1986). As in any social movement begun at the local level, a change-oriented person needs either to be in a place that accepts the fruit of intellectual dissent or to be a steadfast, hardened individual who can proceed despite peer disapproval and possible ostracism. Obviously, it's easier to enlarge the space and pace of change in the company of benign, tolerant, open colleagues than it is if one must deal with persons who seek conformity and resist democratic impulses.

As an individual teacher trying to create a democratic space of one's own, it's important to have a sense of imagination and purpose (Greene, 1995). Teachers must ask themselves, "What would teaching and learning look like, and what would students be able to achieve and demonstrate in my classroom, if democracy were practiced as the most powerful pedagogy of learning for all students?" They can then specify how students can

- Actively work with problems, ideas, materials, and other people as they learn skills and content
- Achieve escalating degrees of choices, both as individuals and as groups, within the parameters provided by the teacher
- Be held accountable before their peers, teachers, parents, and school community to ensure they are using their education time purposefully and productively

- Share their learning with one another, with teachers, and with parents and other community members
- Decide how to make their learning a contribution to their community
- Assume escalating responsibilities for securing resources (such as people and materials outside of the school) and finding places where they can apply and further their learning
- Demonstrate what they know and can do in public settings and receive public feedback
- Work and learn from one another, individually and in groups, at a pace that challenges all

This might mean involving students in setting some of the formats, structures, and rules of learning. It might mean less reliance on textbooks and worksheets and more reliance on reference materials, electronic media, technology, and hands-on activities. It might mean having each student contract for work to be done, with a final demonstration of learning subject to review by peers, parents, and community members. It might mean having all students use what they are learning to tutor younger students or contribute their projects to other schoolwide or community needs. It might mean providing more field experiences for student learning, using community members or parents as teachers. It might mean eliminating homogeneous ability groups, with fuller inclusion of all students. It might mean holding all students to high standards of achievement according to evaluation criteria developed with students, parents, and other faculty. It might mean having students do more of the assessment, planning, and logistical arranging for learning units and projects (through e-mail, phone calls, and written correspondence, and by budgeting and arranging transportation, for example).

Teachers would need to constantly check to see that such innovations do not lead to a purposeless or confused environment conducive to student irresponsibility and academic permissiveness. The evidence suggests, however, that changes toward democratic learning result in increased levels of basic skills, more complete knowledge of various disciplines, and sharpened reasoning skills for use in analyzing, synthesizing, and applying information.

Democracy consists of equality, fraternity, and liberty—qualities that promote freedom. Individual and group choices promote a community that strives for "life, liberty, and the pursuit of happiness" for all. A teacher, in embracing change for greater activity, participation, and responsibility for all students, must clarify how differences in gender, culture, race, socioeconomic status, and religious background can be used to enrich the learning of all. In dealing with such a question, teachers need to confront practices that stereotype, discriminate, or exclude students from full participation.

Maxine Greene has pointed out that by pursuing democratic pedagogy, "a teacher is, in a sense, choosing himself as a rebel against attempts to condition; and it is well for him to do so openly, with full awareness of the responsibility involved as well as of the risks" (1973, p. 171). Carol Lacerenza, a high school teacher, puts it more bluntly: changing toward a pedagogy of democracy does not mean simply realizing that other teachers' practices are contradictory to democracy but also realizing that one's own are as well. One is not simply rebelling against the conditions of education but against one's own strategies as an educator. She says, "There's great trepidation [within and among ourselves as classroom teachers] about a conversation that says 'I really stink at this. I need to think differently. . . . Can you help me?' That's a difficult conversation to start, and we can't get at all of those systemic issues until that conversation can thrive" (Wolk & Rodman, 1994, p. 198).

So whether the conversation begins within a single teacher's mind or within a larger context with colleagues and an entire school community, there needs to be a conscious space for teachers to rebel, in thought and in action.

LOCATING THE PROBLEM AND THE POTENTIAL FOR CHANGE

The lack of responsiveness to purposeful democratic change on the part of many teachers is reasonable when viewed in the historical context of the waves of mandated innovations that have been exhorted and prescribed by educational experts, state legislatures, superintendents, and "blue ribbon commissions." Such waves of "top-down" change appear to experienced teachers to be periodic and endless. If one waits long enough—until the current superintendent leaves, the commission report becomes old, or another innovation captures the media's attention—then the current mandated reform shall pass (see Sarason, 1990, 1996). Teachers, principals, and schools have a built-in resiliency to such innovations and "swallow" such practices into their previous practice and routines (Cuban, 1989, 1993). The legacy of public education is a hierarchical, control-oriented structure: the district controls the schools, the administrators and unions control the teachers, and the teachers control the students. Furthermore, most teachers, administrators, teacher educators, parents, and community members rarely think seriously about democracy in terms of the content and process of education, as a way of learning and living. Instead, if the word *democracy* is used at all, it is used as an abstract, patriotic term related to the nation's might, representative government, or individual liberty, or it is simply a placeholder in mission and vision statements. So, to really define the word and to put it into operation as a learning strategy has to create some confusion and pain; it will never lead to a "correct solution" but instead to continual conversations and different applications.

It is not surprising, then, that so many teachers, classrooms, and schools are the way they are: nondemocratic in thought and action. Teachers themselves went to classrooms and schools predicated on control; their own teacher preparation was learned in university or college programs predicated on the same hierarchy of authority and passivity. Therefore, the question of the relationship between democracy and education is not part of the "lived experience" of current teachers and teacher educators (or, for that matter, most Americans). So, a normal explanation by teachers—whether in public or private schools; at the elementary, middle, or secondary level; or in colleges, universities, or vocational centers—when students aren't learning as well as they would like them to learn can be summed up in the words of teacher Carol Lacerenza: "The consensus is that the clientele needs to change. . . . All . . . is blamed on the portion of our community [parents and students] who [do] not come to the party with the right equipment. There is not a universal acceptance of the notion that we need to change. In fact, there's a universal resistance" (Wolk & Rodman, 1994, pp. 190–191).

The intent here is not to blame teachers and educators for the nondemocratic practices of our classrooms and schools—very few people are consciously antidemocratic. Blame can be equally shared among teachers' unions, school boards, state legislators, colleges and universities, corporate heads, governors, federalists, parents, local citizens, educational reformers, and policymakers. The lack of serious discussion and efforts to practice democracy as education is the fault of all of us, and we are all potentially part of the solution of creating a more congruent, participatory, and improved education for all. Yet such mobilization will not happen by itself. Someone—some person, school, district, or community—has to step out and take the lead with words to this effect: "What I (we) currently do is probably no worse or better than what has been done in the past, but it's not good enough. What I (we) will do in the future is to take education and democracy seriously so that all students learn to excel." For democracy as education to work, it has to be understood as a return to the most enduring and conservative idea of a people—not as simply another innovation to be laid over existing programs. Democracy cannot be imposed by hierarchical mandates, but it does need inspired leadership and support for it to become a reality.

It is from such stepping out by individuals and groups that the American Revolution was born, women's suffrage was gained, child labor laws were enacted, and civil rights were won, and it is how many major advances in education have been made (Wolk & Rodman, 1994; Cremin, 1964; Zinn, 1980; Ayers, 1995). One teacher launches an activist organization of teachers that influences an entire large urban district; another teacher creates a way of bringing writing and literature to children that spreads into thousands of classrooms across the nation; another educator refuses to accept that poor minority children are low achievers and shows hundreds of others how to reverse such low expectations. The ideas of a few curious schools to rethink the entire structure of schooling creates a proliferation of school renewal networks that have provided support to change practices in thousands of schools in America.[1]

Strength will ensue when we as educational professionals admit publicly that we do not know how to educate as well as we all wish and that as professionals we need to constantly plan how to do better (see Pogrow, 1996; Fullan & Stiegelbauer, 1991). Weakness will ensue if we act as if we know all there is to know about how to educate well, defend what is currently being done as the best under the circumstances, and then treat students, parents, citizens, and other laypersons as visitors rather than members of the educational enterprise (Mathews, 1996). It is no wonder that community members, parents, and other laypeople have come to distrust educators and have, in some places, created storms of protests against being excluded from decisions about education (see Lasch, 1995). So, a place to begin as an individual educator is with one's own room and one's own students, peers, school, and community.

LEADERSHIP FOR CHANGE

Most of my professional life—as a teacher, principal, and university–public school collaborator—has been devoted to studying and acting on classroom and school change. There is no cookbook of prescriptive steps for successful change. Success is a process of making informed decisions toward reaching a desired end rather than a series of steps to be followed. The following are some suggestions for agents of change to consider as they move toward the practices of democracy as education.

Classroom-Level Leadership

SUGGESTION 1. Change needs to be public. Students, parents, principals, and colleagues need to be openly informed about the why and what of changes being made in one's classroom. Postman and Weingartner (1971) once wrote that teaching was a subversive activity; but if it is so subversive that others cannot understand, critique, and participate in what a classroom teacher is doing, then there is no reciprocity for gaining support to change anyone else's practice. As mentioned, one needs a space of one's own; it may be relatively private for a while, but eventually others need to know what is occurring and the reasons for why the classroom might be looking different from others. This openness about one's space helps create a norm that it is acceptable for colleagues to tell, ask, and deliberate about the purpose and reasons for what is occurring in theirs and others' classrooms.

SUGGESTION 2. Seek out colleagues—teachers, parents, and school leaders—as peer coaches and critical friends. Find at least one other person in your school to critique, observe, and solve problems with you around activities and assessments of student performance. Ask parents and community members to become involved inside and outside your classroom as resource persons, to help students demonstrate what they are learning and to make suggestions regarding how students might apply their learning in their home, job, and community. Ask parents and community persons to offer feedback on classroom activities and student assessments and suggestions for improving students' learning.

SUGGESTION 3. Understand at a personal level that change involves recursive human decisions within an environment of competing tensions and predicaments and that it rarely results in an "Aha!" utopian breakthrough by which students always accomplish excellent work. Democracy as education is always purposeful, but it is less predictable from moment to moment. As a result, inclusiveness and participation of students in classroom activities can create awkward moments (for example, a student unexpectedly asks a teacher for his or her own views on a politically charged, controversial issue in the school, and the teacher is momentarily at a loss as to how to reply; a student is encouraged to make her own learning arrangements and when doing so inadvertently offends a powerful community member; students complain about their teacher's reasserting authority over their poor classroom work and challenge her with, "Hey, I thought this is a democracy—how come we can't do what we want?"; a parent walks in unannounced and complains in front of the entire class that her son isn't being taught anything; students exercise what they believe to be their freedom of expression by being rude to a person who looks and acts differently from them). The constant leadership dilemma of a change-oriented teacher is when to assert authority, when to lessen it, and when to challenge students. These are not simple to predetermine, and many times occurrences with students, parents, and peers do not have clear and immediate resolutions. So to acknowledge this unpredictability with others and to ask for progress checks with students, parents, and colleagues concerning how all is going and how students are learning not only lessens defensiveness among these parties but also is essential for further self-corrections and student progress.

School-Level Leadership

The ideal situation for changes in teaching and learning is in a school where all members have developed and share the same beliefs about their total organization—core beliefs about education; rules of decision making for planning and implementing changes in curricula, instruction, staff development, and assessment; and ongoing action research to study changes and assess impacts on student learning. I have written extensively about these three dimensions of school renewal—the covenant, the charter, and the critical study process—in a previous book (Glickman, 1993) and will not take up additional space discussing them here. Instead, I wish to extend that work and offer some suggestions that a school leader (principal, teacher, leader, or department head) might use in being a schoolwide change agent for democratic pedagogy.

SUGGESTION 1. Challenge the school community to examine and explain what is meant by the word *democracy* and how it applies to schools and education. Many schools in America have written a mission statement or vision statement for their school that uses this word. To ask faculty, parents, staff, students, and others to "unpack" that word into educational and operational terms will create an awareness that the school has a responsibility larger than each individual teacher's preferences for autonomy in his or her own classroom. The discussion will help all members move beyond the popular notions that democracy simply means majority rule, individual liberty, or free-market systems.

SUGGESTION 2. After examining the word in faculty meetings, with parents, and with students, ask for examples and counterexamples of curricula, grouping, teaching and learning methods, and assessments that are congruent—or incongruent—with the definition of democracy. Ask people to be specific and to give practical examples, and ask for a public rationale as to why the practice fits. Provide opportunities for others to discuss whether they agree or do not agree with the examples and rationales offered. It is typically better to ask members to begin with examples, vignettes, or case studies of classrooms and schools outside their own. This is one reason why networking with other schools is quite helpful. To critique the teaching and learning practices of other classrooms and schools initially creates less defensiveness and more open discussions (it's easier to talk about what others do wrong before we talk about what we do wrong). The next phase then would be to discuss examples within our own classrooms and programs in our own school in a manner (and with ground rules) that encourages and models critical, serious, civil, and at times playful talk with one another.

SUGGESTION 3. Establish, through a participatory decision-making process, what actual demonstrations of democratic pedagogy would look like in terms of student achievement—for all students, across all levels of the school—and how they would be publicly assessed. What should students be able to do when they leave the school, and how will they demonstrate such learning in a way that will satisfy the school? It might take several years to plan, implement, and evaluate a schoolwide policy for demonstrating student learning, but the school will then have a pedagogical direction for everyone who works with its students.

With the schools that compose the League of Professional Schools, we have begun such a process for deriving such demonstrations of practices within and across elementary, middle, and secondary schools. These are the questions that we began with:

1. *What does it mean to be a democratic school?* Does it mean that democracy is only for professionals and not for others, or can democracy and professionalism complement each other? What should be the rules for parents, students, community members, and district representatives? What decisions should educators mostly concern themselves with, and what other decisions should be made by others, for purposes of expediency, expertise, and responsibility.

2. *What is democracy?* Is democracy governance and decision-making procedures only, or is it a way of learning and living together among all those who attend and work in a school? Does a school show its belief in democracy by using curricula and instruction in ways that demand more involvement, participation, choices, and contributions of students?

3. *What does a democratic school look like?* Imagine five years from now what a classroom and school would look like if they were truly democratic. What would an observer see? What would be the school's decision-making processes? What would the day-to-day curricula, schedules, and student activities look like across the school? How would action research be used to establish internal schoolwide demonstrations and standards of student learning?

4. *What do all students learn in a democratic and professional school, and how is it demonstrated, assessed, and measured?* All student learning in League schools should involve comprehensive and ongoing participation, application of learning, connection between school members, contribution, and responsibility. What should be the assessment standards of such purposeful student learning? What should students be able to demonstrate? How and by whom should such demonstrations be assessed?

Parent- and Community-Level Leadership

As a parent or community member, one has the right and responsibility to be involved in the education of one's own children as well as the children of the entire community. There is not a unilateral right to impose one's own view of education on others in a school, but there is a right to be involved as a participant, to have voice and influence in the direction taken educating the community's youth. The public school is, after all, public, and everyone is part of the public—in terms of financial support, citizenship, and purpose. Thus if one's own child's classrooms and schools do not embrace democratic education, one can legitimately ask of educators, Why not? One can offer to be part of articulating a clearer mission for the school and be involved in problem solving and implementation. A parent or community member can request meetings, discussions, and open forums and can insist that parents and community persons have real roles in making decisions about education beyond the perfunctory roles of fundraising, arranging refreshments for open houses, or extracurricular "booster clubs." A citizen can invite other parents and community members who have the same questions and wish to participate. If classrooms are routinized, passive, joyless, and unimaginative, then citizens should be change agents for democratic learning, opening discussions about their schools' practices with teachers and other school officials.

Dewey once wrote that what a parent wants for his or her own child he or she should also want for all children (1968, p. 3). For example, parents and citizens should be able to ask such questions as "Why do some students get more time on computers, more challenging and engaging curricula, and more projects and self-directed learning than others?" And they should expect reasonable explanations from professionals and have the ability to participate in making changes in their classrooms, schools, and district.

In the past, parents and community members have changed schools and created new schools as a result of asking such questions and becoming active (Mathews, 1996; Derene, 1996; Study Circles Resource Center, 1995). For every success story, there are other stories of parent and community members being patronized, avoided, or ignored by school officials and faculty. The separation of schools from parents and community have led in some cases to community apathy or resignation and in other cases to a few of the most vocal and powerful parents redirecting school practices to serve their own narrow interests. Or sometimes a school simply finds a single teacher to respond to parents and citizens concerned about democratic education. The fact that parents, citizens, and professional educators are not often involved in school partnerships, though the need for it is widely identified, is not always due to the unresponsiveness of educators; in some cases it is the failure of parents, citizens, and business members to find the time to be involved. It's always easier to criticize what others are doing than to be part of the process of determining what should be done instead. Also, it is hardly a secret that in virtually all communities there are members, including parents, who are rude to others, aggregate individual power for personal gain, and are unwilling to listen to the reasons and explanations of others.

Not all parent and community member demands are prodemocratic in intent (they might often be the reverse), and not all school and classroom practices are hostile, discriminatory, and passive (some can be more egalitarian, inclusive, and active than some highly influential parents want classrooms and schools to be). The point is that public education in a democracy has a responsibility to provide an education that is challenging to all students. This can only be done through the invitation, deliberations, and decisions of all those who care about schools. Such a process of democratic conversation is the means for achieving democratic practices and purposes in a school.

To summarize, leadership for change should operate at multiple levels. Individual teachers should forge ahead in their own classrooms, school leaders should press the issues of democracy in the larger community, and parents and citizens should challenge classroom teachers and school officials to be democratic. At every level, what is being created are expanding public spaces that might begin in semiprivate rooms that eventually bring force to bear on the entire school.

—⁓—

We have all read in history books about the great heroes of America who have changed history. We mythologize these leaders—presidents, generals, social rights reformers, scientists, teachers, and theological visionaries. What is missing or incomplete about these histories is that, first, they fail to acknowledge that such heroes were ordinary people who battled self-doubt and frustrations and erred almost as often as they succeeded, and that, second, for every hero publicly acknowledged, there have been hundreds and thousands of others who made similar efforts to correct injustice and better their communities for all people.[2] It is this second group of individuals, who never sought credit and rarely received it, who understood that to live democratically means confronting hypocrisy in oneself and in others. It means doing something about it.

Notes

1. I'm referring here to such networks as the Coalition of Essential Schools, the Accelerated Schools, the Success for All Schools, the Comer Schools, the National Center for Restructuring Schools and Teaching, the New American School Design Teams, the Annenberg Lead School Project, and the League of Professional Schools.
2. A number of examples of current democratic activism by such people as Joe Caldwell, Mimi Kaplan, and Theresa Francis can be found in Lappé & Martin, 1994.

—⁓— Listening to Students

"Y ou have to know the kids. They teach me how to teach them. They may be from all kinds of backgrounds and cultures, but if you really listen to them, they'll tell you how to teach them" (Delpit, 1994, p. 120). When we hold large conferences for educators that include concurrent sessions, those sessions that are usually packed and most highly favored are the ones that feature students (elementary, middle, or secondary) describing their significant learning experiences in classrooms and schools. The students conclude such presentations with suggestions to teachers and administrators as to what they could do to change their own practices to help their own students learn better. Overhearing the conversations of attendees as they leave such presentations is both encouraging and perplexing. One hears teachers and principals rave about the insights and reality of what these students say. They often note on their conference assessment forms that they learned more from the students than from the national experts flown in from afar to give keynote addresses. Yet what is puzzling to me is that these students who capture such attention are just like students that the attendees have every day in their own classrooms and schools. They really don't have to go to a conference to listen to them. It simply doesn't occur to many of us to ask the same questions and gather the same suggestions from our own students.

Young children, adolescents, teenagers, or adults—students in all classrooms and schools across all subject areas have definite ideas about their education. Why do so many educators not ask or listen to their own students discuss issues and practices of education? The only answer that I can surmise is that, outside of ignorance (which I don't think to be the case), if we ask our own students for input, they will tell us what we might prefer not to know. To not know means not having to act. If asked, students will tell us what is wonderful and engaging as well as what is boring, shoddy, and disrespectful. They will clearly explain what teachers do to inspire their best work, but they also will explain what teachers do to bring out the worst in them.

Wasley, Hampel, and Clark shadowed students in reform-oriented schools for three years, and they uncovered a dichotomy. School faculty complained that their students were apathetic, irresponsible, made little effort, and were always expecting to be entertained. The same students in these classrooms confided to the researchers that their teachers were inept. According to one female student, "It's just the same old thing. I go to class, and we do what we do almost every day. . . . It's just so boring." Another student referred to by his teacher as apathetic said, "I don't do all the work because a lot of it seems like busy work. . . . Sometimes, it feels like he gives us the work to keep us busy rather than because it is important for us to know" (1997). These students, who were constantly labeled as students who made no effort (some received good grades, some did not), expressed that their behavior was totally different in classrooms with teachers who came to class prepared, interested, and ready to push, who respected students and took their intellectual exchanges seriously, and who truly enjoyed their company.

It would appear to be just common sense for educators to listen to their own students, but the risks of doing so are often perceived as high. In our own private conversations with students, they tell us about what is helping them learn—they cite particular projects, lessons, and ways of presenting materials. They talk about good teachers and teaching, but they also tell us just as clearly about the other side. Students have openly told us about growing hostility and discrimination between students and teachers around gender, race, and socioeconomic class, within individual classrooms and throughout entire schools. Students have told us of long-standing sexual harassment by a teacher and about how when students raised the issue it was ignored by the teacher, other faculty, and administrators. Students have reported to us on drug usage and physical intimidation. In several instances what students said about what they have experienced in their school has contradicted what the adults in the school say ("We have few or none of these problems here"). Of course, it is possible that students might be distorting and exaggerating, and all incidents are considered allegations until verified. Public knowledge of unverified claims could lead to a manufactured crisis and harm among colleagues, parents, and school boards.

I don't wish to make light of the matter of asking students what they think. Virtually everyone who devotes their lives to a career believes that what they are doing, they are doing well. Without critique or data, the comfort of continuing perceptions of one's own success is kept intact. But refusing examination of one's work by students (and others) has great cost. Many students will not learn as well as they could, and furthermore, students learn from the refusal of teachers to gather and listen to student feedback that they do not really value the democratic ideals of freedom, inquiry, and free dissemination of information. Students learn that what is real for adults is the protection of their egos and self-image.

The fact that most of us as adults do not typically seek information about our performance is not due to any inherent character flaw but instead attributable to how we learned as students and later as adults to survive in a world of power—in schools and in work. Most teachers were fairly good students—defined as being obedient; knowing when to smile; learning the game concerning when to initiate or defer, depending on the teacher's clues; and knowing how to keep teachers' authority, self importance, and ego intact. By figuring out what the teacher wanted, we learned to gain the teacher's approval and the desired grade, reward, or recognition. Thus, to lower our guard, to loose our control over information, and to self-correct are actions that go against what we have learned about how to successfully gain comfort and security in a world dominated by authority. However, Sarason (1996) has noted that healthy individuals and healthy organizations are not in the mode of self-preservation but in the mode of self-correction—always gathering data, assessing, validating, critiquing, and adjusting according to progress made toward goals.

My experience as a university instructor might be instructive as to why our current conditions exist—why student feedback is not openly solicited and what an individual can expect when trying to rectify the balance of power between teachers and students in creating an intellectual community where all members are held to standards of important learning. In giving my personal experience as a teacher, I might exaggerate successes on my part and downplay the failures. I'll try to be honest, and I hope that my past and current students and colleagues will continue to provide me with an honest rendering of what occurs in the name of good and poor learning. Furthermore, I do not equate my experience of teaching in a public university setting with teaching in a public school setting of young children, adolescents, and young adults. Teaching older students who have all experienced traditional academic success and have chosen and been admitted to a college or university is substantially different from teaching younger students who have a greater range of behaviors, attitudes, and academic experiences and have no choice but to attend. Public school (preschool through twelfth grade) teaching is much more challenging than university teaching in the range of management, teaching, and learning decisions required. (For explanations and descriptions of teachers' successfully using student feedback at public school levels and settings, see Fried, 1995; Ladson-Billings, 1994; Wood, 1992; Wolk & Rodman, 1994).

For most courses that I teach,[1] whether through team teaching or alone, I bring to the class an incomplete syllabus that includes

- A course description
- Description of course content—skills, knowledge, and understandings—to be learned
- Central questions of the course
- List of readings and some assignments, including a community service or field experience requirement and a team project
- Expectations for assessment, evaluation, and grades

On the first day, I tell students why we are there—that we've agreed to come together for so many hours and weeks to learn about a topic that we might not normally learn if we were left to our own devices. I then use a teaching method learned and adopted from my years of involvement with the Foxfire Network in Georgia, a method used in public and private classrooms in all content fields and all grade levels (see Wigginton, 1985). I ask students to write individually about the most positive, memorable learning experiences they have had in school, at whatever level. I then ask them to read their written descriptions to each other in pairs, and then I move them into larger groups for discussion. I ask each group to identify from their collection of individual experiences with positive learning what are the characteristics of a good classroom, a good teacher, and good students. After doing so and soliciting their findings, I ask them to define for me what good students are able to achieve, demonstrate, or show at the end of a course when they have "learned exceptionally well the content of the course." The following is a summary of the common characteristics generated by my most recent undergraduate class of students.

Course, Spring 1996

Characteristics of a good classroom:

- Discussions
- Respect for individual students
- Positive reinforcement
- Out-of-classroom experiences—variety
- Flexibility concerning needs and wants of students
- Sharing of experiences among students
- Ability of teacher to learn from students
- Good attitude from class
- Involvement of students
- Variety of teaching methods
- No negative reinforcement or motivation
- Disciplined—orderly, respectful
- Changes in environment—varied format
- Structure, to create a comfort zone

Characteristics of a good teacher:

- Earns respect
- Sets rules—time to learn and time for fun
- Makes students feel special
- Finds creative ways to learn

- Doesn't stereotype students
- Listens to what students have to say

Characteristics of an effective student:
- Alert, attentive
- Open-minded
- Responsible
- Willing to learn
- Conscientious
- Considerate and respectful of teacher and others
- Confident of own ability
- Motivated
- Involved in learning
- Willing to interact with others

What students should be able to demonstrate:
- Evidence of having synthesized and analyzed the readings, class activities, community service, and field experiences according to the central questions of the course, through communicating (orally, graphically, or in writing) what has been the theoretical or abstract problems presented in the course and how they can be solved with clarity, logic, and reasoning.
- An application of a solution to these problems in an actual situation at the local, state, national, or international level.

Students tend to enjoy doing these activities, and after they have finished I tell them that I will rework their list to include my expectations and we will complete our course syllabus with mutual standards of practice and assessment. We then spend another three hours over the next few class days to complete the syllabus. In the interim, I tell them to do the readings and activities assigned, and I organize each class period during the first half of the course. At the conclusion of the very first class, I ask if students have questions. Most students stare at me or shrug their shoulders, but a few students are brave enough to mention the inevitable question, "What do we need to do to get an A?" I answer that my expectations for an A can be found in the syllabus and will be based on a student's doing excellent work as defined by our joint expectations and standards of quality. Furthermore, I tell them that as a class we will differentiate, together, student work that is judged excellent, good, average, or poor.

For the next six weeks, I give some lectures, organize panel forums, help them individually develop their community learning contracts with me, and hold many discussions around their assigned readings—in small and in large groups. I scan these discussions to see that everyone has the opportunity to be involved, and I alter discussion formats depending on the degree of participation from students. In discussions, I try to accept all of their contributions and ideas, and I keep pushing them to explain their perspective by asking them to make reference to the readings as well as their own experiences. I also insist that they give me more than their opinions—that they give me the reasons behind their opinions, so that I and their classmates can understand them. After the first few weeks, during discussions, I move out of their direct line of sight and have them direct their talk to one another rather than to me. From time to time, I ask them to write thought pieces, and I give them a few short quizzes (as outlined in the initial syllabus). Occasionally I review at the beginning or end of class what we agreed were the criteria of a good teacher, a good student, and a good classroom. I remind them that we need to hold ourselves personally and collectively accountable for meeting these criteria.

At midpoint of our course schedule and after detecting confusions and grumblings about the class and the grades that they are receiving on their quizzes and assignments, I have us stop as a class and relook at our mutual criteria. I ask them individually and privately to write down on paper "how you, I, and we are doing in regard to our criteria of a good student, good teacher, and good classroom." I assure them of anonymity (they are told not to write their names on their paper, and I pledge not to do any detective work). After they write down their individual reactions, I ask them to share within a small group and ask a group reporter, of their choosing, to report to me and the entire class what individuals (again anonymously) have said.

Although from the very first class I make a point to talk informally with students before, during, and after class; in passing in the halls; and at office hours, where I encourage drop-in visits, I never really find out what they think about the class until I stop and take classroom time to formally do so. And when I formally ask, and they tell me, no matter how often I have done this in the past, I'm never prepared for their critical appraisal. I know intellectually that students can learn well without thinking that I'm a nice person, but still, I often get my feelings hurt. Here are examples of their unedited comments:

> "I feel like this class has been a waste of my time. I don't feel like I have learned anything and I have attended every class. I feel we just talk back and forth and never learn what you want us to. I would not advise anyone to take this class!! . . . Your teaching is not very good."

> "One of the characteristics of a good teacher is to 'prepare students for examinations.' This has not been done at all. I wish the class was more structured."

> "This is not how I expected this class to be. I wish this class was more straightforward."

> "Instructor is very opinionated and fails to present both sides of an issue."

> "I wish there was more facts, more lectures. The instructor is too theoretical, vague, dry, and boring."

Other students responded that I was "too liberal," and others stated that they never knew where I stood on an issue. And finally, one student remarked that as an instructor I had an "eccentric style." There were a number of positive comments to help balance the negatives, such as "I do feel you are intelligent and have much to offer, but your teaching needs more structure." What I was trying to glean from these responses was information that (1) could make me a more effective teacher, (2) could make students take more responsibility for their own learning, and (3) would make us all problem solvers concerning how to make the course better, so that we could document that substantial and valuable learning would transpire.

Up until this point in the course, the activities I had done with them in the first class and over the first few weeks to develop standards of practice and complete the syllabus had been seen by most of them as simply a simulation exercise. They truly didn't believe that what they were doing was something that we actually would adhere to. So, when this midterm assessment of me and the class was finished, I reminded them that this was "our" class, we all had responsibilities in it, and I was asking them and myself to reflect on the information presented (including my comments, both positive and negative, about individual student performances and the class as a whole). I directed them to come back for the next class with plans of action, and I told them I would do the same. Mine would be about becoming a better teacher, theirs should be about becoming better students, and both of ours would be about how to become a better community of learners. Many left that day skeptical about doing such an assignment, thinking that I as a teacher still "just didn't get it." (However, one male student who had been very quiet through the first half of the course pulled me aside after class and said that when I told the class that we are all adults and we couldn't make learning better unless we really talked to one another honestly, those words really hit him. He candidly confessed to me that after the first few quizzes, he figured that he couldn't get an A and thus had lost incentive and was just sliding by to pass the course. He realized now that he had been acting irresponsibly, had been treating the course as a game to get a grade, not as an education, and now wanted to talk about being more responsible.)

That one day of formal assessment turned the course around for me and for most of the students. Students and I came to the next class with our improvement plans. We agreed that I would lecture more and give clearer directions. They would assume responsibility for some group presentations over agreed-upon topics and provide activities that would vary from my previous teaching formats. Finally, we agreed to construct together a final examination that would be fair and rigorous and would use weights and rubrics for scoring.

The second half of the course was quite different from the first. One group of students spent several nights producing a video to illustrate universal concerns about pedagogy. Another group gained access to an interactive distance laboratory and utilized visual artists to show the advantages and disadvantages of technology in education. Another group created a television format to debate the controversial issues of education. Prior to final papers and exams, they developed a system of coaching each other on their drafts of written responses to the core questions of the course. At the end they generated a comprehensive set of closed- and open-book questions about what every student should be able to answer, and then I selected from the questions for the final exam.

I asked my university colleagues who teach the same course to review the exam questions developed by the students. My colleagues concluded that the degree of difficulty was far beyond what they normally expect in their own classes, and one even asked me if it was fair to expect so much from my students. My answer was that we as a class had decided that it was fair to hold ourselves to such standards.

So did I succeed, or not? At the end, not many students received A's, but I did see greater involvement, enthusiasm, and deeper thinking on the part of students than I see in most university classes where the course belongs solely to the instructor. Other faculty would drop in from time to time to observe this "unusual" class, and one student invited her mother to attend. After the last class session, we conducted a final assessment of the course to help me organize for the next time I would teach it. The following are a selection of their anonymous and unedited responses:

"I was more permanently and universally affected by the class discussion we had on the first Monday of the second half of the quarter. That day you sat us down and asked us what we thought about the class and we told you. I have never before had a teacher open himself up to such criticism and I have never had a teacher accept such criticism from students."

"The second half of this course was quite different from the first. I am used to abiding by unchanging rules that the teacher makes because he or she knows best. Now, all that talk about democracy, education, Jefferson, and liberty-equality-fraternity finally make sense."

"I could tell something was different and special about this class. . . . We had some problems and difficulties between teachers and students. I found it to be particularly sensitive and noble that a teacher would give so much effort and place so much importance in considering student ideas rather than imposing one's beliefs on a class. This experience changed my life and the importance I place on teaching, learning, and education."

"I have had many memorable experiences in my school career, both good and bad, which have led me to want to be a teacher. However, it was not until midpoint of this quarter that I found the true definition of being a good teacher. I finally figured out what it was about those great teachers in high school or elementary school. . . . They led democratic classrooms, ones which catered to everyone, open to new ideas, and make the student feel welcome."

"This course has changed my way of thinking about education. I thought those first few days were kind of silly but now I know *we* were a part of this class. I look around the room and see familiar faces that I have shared my thoughts and ideas. We were forced to become involved in learning not just for ourselves but for the good of everyone. It seems so strange (after fourteen years of being a student) that almost all my teachers have overlooked such a beneficial way of learning."

I keep copies of many of the students' final products. I show them to other colleagues and give them as examples for future students. But, to be honest, there continued to be students who did not like the class and/or me to the extreme. And despite the high praise of some students for my teaching, I know that I'm not a great teacher. I'm not a well-organized lecturer with a dynamic delivery. In discussions that I lead, I have a tendency to ramble. I'm forever having to remind myself to focus on content and not spend undue time on process, and the directions I give students are often unclear. I'm aware that I need to be more diligent about responding quickly to students' written assignments. And I need to become more current in some of the fields in which I teach. And last, my humor is often funny only to me, and narrating my own personal experiences are often not of much interest to undergraduate students. So even though I've been recognized by students and faculty for my teaching, no one should ever equate me with the great teachers in universities, public schools, and other education settings.

Teachers such as Corla Hawkins, who works in a destitute urban middle school, or the thousands like her who teach in our public schools in all types of settings listen to and act with their students in acutely more insightful ways (Kozol, 1991, p. 47). They have patience, organizational skills, clarity of speech, and mastery of content beyond mine. So what I find so striking about my teaching and why it appears to be life changing for many students is simply that what they experience with me is novel. They rarely have prior experience of teachers treating them with the recognition, attention, and consideration that any respectful adult would confer upon another. After all, what I simply do is check with them, call them at home when pleased or displeased with their work, and listen to them in ways that I would want people to listen to me. I try to use my authority as a teacher to see that they learn well. I don't do everything they want. I get annoyed at them, and they get annoyed at me. But above all else, I'm responsible, as bell hooks (1995, p. 153) says, for creating a learning context that we are all committed to.

In many ways it is sad that these students have such praise for my methods of asking them for their ideas and acting upon them; it shows how rare these approaches are in education. Students who have not experienced such a setting in their entire school career and then become teachers don't have any lived experience of democracy as education. As hooks points out, even those who have made stellar careers out of the study and espousal of inclusiveness, deconstruction, constructivism, feminism, postmodernism, liberation, and empowerment and have continually embraced new ways of thinking are still too often "attached to old ways of *practicing teaching*" (p. 142).

STUDENT RESPONSIBILITY

There is a reciprocal obligation between students and teachers. The power is clearly not equal, but students have a responsibility to press the issue of influence with their teachers in an effort to improve their learning. The typical strategy in classrooms and schools for involving students is to ask them to handle peripheral matters such as deciding what the school colors should be, organizing the prom, holding fundraisers, and voting in class on whether they want to have free time now or later. What I have discussed in this essay is not influence on the periphery but influence on the core issues of education—teaching and learning, curriculum development, and assessment. If students are bold enough—and aren't immediately removed from a classroom or school for doing so—they need to ask for and suggest ways they can become involved with their teachers and administrators in determining how to improve learning. At a school level, sympathetic peers, teachers, and administrators can help by putting such issues on the agenda of school councils and student government. Assuredly, power in classrooms and schools should not be shared equally between teachers and students in all matters, but how to learn is a matter best informed by all those involved. Even the rejection of such an issue by a classroom teacher or school creates public awareness that there *is* an issue and opens the possibility of further pursuing it.

Last, it is important that educators, parents, and community members understand that I'm not advocating student-run classrooms or student-run schools. I'm not advocating parity between students and adults on all matters. Teachers should have more authority and responsibility, based on their experience and wisdom, to determine students' educational experiences. Not all student ideas are good—some students might make dishonest, vindictive, naive, or unworkable plans; some students might see teachers' asking for their feedback as a way of avoiding hard work. But the same can be said of educators' ideas—some are purposeful, others are not. It is the responsibility of an educational institution fulfilling democratic purposes to see that as much information and ideas for improvement as possible be solicited, entertained, and studied, in the widest possible forums, before further decisions are made to improve education. A critical source of such valuable information and ideas passes by us every day in our own classrooms and schools.

Note

1. I'm referring here to classes of under forty-five students. I do teach an occasional course with several hundred students. I have to use a much different organizational plan to increase participation, involvement, and facilitation with such large numbers. I omit such a discussion because most educators do not teach such large groups, and the details of what I do, with varying degrees of success, would be quite lengthy.

—∿— Leadership for Democracy

Democracy means having a say, being personally connected to important decisions that are made about the community that I spend substantial time in. Democracy, to me, means living in and being responsible for and being helped by a community. We get to make decisions because (the school in this case) is ours. We have to take care of it for precisely the same reason, and I know that I would take care of a Mom and Pop bodega in a different sort of way than I would a McDonald's—because it is mine.

And I believe that members of a community—a community that they have some ownership of, a democratic community—have the potential of treating each other differently than in a traditional institution. There can be an identification based on community that will not happen in a huge impersonal institution (where people are known by roles and status, not Paul, Carl and Christine), active in good faith members of our school [Paul Schwarz, personal communication, December 27, 1995].

These words, written to me by the codirector of Central Park East Secondary School in New York City—one of the most noted and successful secondary schools in the United States and a demonstration site of the Coalition of Essential Schools—convey similar sentiments to those articulated by teachers, administrators, students, and parents who have participated in the schools (elementary, middle, and secondary) that have been long-term members of the League of Professional Schools (see Allen & Glickman, 1997; Lunsford, 1995). As a veteran parent narrated to me after six years of school effort, "We could never go back. . . . This school now belongs to all of us."

These people view democracy as a way for all community members to relate, learn, and live together. Contrary to conventional lore about democracy's being inefficient (or, to summarize Winston Churchill, "the worst possible system except for all the rest"), they don't see democracy and participation as messy and inefficient. Instead, they see equalizing roles and status and distributing control as the most efficient and best ways of ensuring that all students learn well. To them, democracy is not laissez faire. It is not an abdication of authority and responsibility. Instead, it is the creation of more power all around and greater accountability for what all students should be able to know and do.

However, for most educators and citizens, the central tenets of democracy—equality, liberty, and fraternity; life, liberty, and the pursuit of happiness—are not commonly understood, articulated, or implemented. (Regardless of how the word *democracy* is used in written mission and policy statements, it is usually a word like *motherhood* and *apple pie,* without any deeper explanation). There have been perennial debates about the purpose of education (see Ravitch, 1983; Spring, 1996; Cremin, 1964). Those on the political extremes believe schools should serve either unrestricted liberty or unwavering, flag-waving patriotism. There are others who believe education should be about jobs, vocations, careers, private enterprise, and the economy, as opposed to an instrument for promoting social reconstruction, environmental health, or critiques of imperialist America. And then there are the battles among secularists and religionists concerning whether the schools should suppress or advocate religious beliefs and values. And, finally, there are the vast majority of citizens and parents, who simply want schools to be safe, disciplined, and caring places where children are taught basic skills, reasoning skills, tolerance, and civility so that they will have choices later in life about leisure, work, community involvement, and further education (Johnson & Immerwahr, 1994).

It is this large group of individual parents and citizens who refuse to have ideologies described for them by political parties, religious organizations, or other groups. And when this group is made conscious of how democracy as education can be the most powerful way of learning and living for their children, then understanding, consensus, and change in public schools and education can be achieved. The others, those with egos tied to dogmatic beliefs, will continue to throw ideological bombs at one another. The only benefit of rigid ideological thinking is that it allows the large group of open-minded people to determine the range of alternatives between the polarized positions. They then can deliberate with reason and make up their own minds.

The role of a facilitator is to lead discussions by encouraging the honest expression of all points of view in a safe and respectful environment, to convey one's own views, and to stimulate decisions by an agreed-upon process that satisfy agreed-upon goals—in this case the goal of providing a public education that allows greater equality, liberty, and fraternity for all students. When decisions move away from the criteria of equality, liberty, and fraternity—including democratically made decisions that are undemocratic in spirit (for example, by closing off equality, hardening lines of student access, protecting stratification and privilege, or keeping students passive and isolated)—then, and only then, does a change agent ask for review and, if necessary, appeal to other authorities (school boards, accrediting agencies, state authorities, and the courts) or go outside unresponsive authority structures and directly to the people (through the media and public protests).

A courageous example of discussion, review, appeal, and resistance can be found in the recent case of Calhoun County, Georgia, superintendent Corkin Cherubini (White, 1996). Cherubini, a high school teacher for twenty-two years in the Calhoun school system, was troubled by what he saw as the unjust placement of students, from an early age, into separate, tracked classes of ability groups divided along racial lines. Upon becoming superintendent, he studied the evidence and found that African American students with higher achievement scores than white students were being systematically placed in lower-track classes, and white students with lower scores were being placed in higher-track classes. This practice of tracking in subtle and not-so-subtle ways to separate students by race, class, and family background can be found in other schools and districts across the United States (see Oakes & Guiton, 1995). However, Cherubini refused to ignore it, and he held discussions with the schools, community, and school board about the matter. When it became apparent that no progress on this issue would be made, he notified the U.S. Department of Justice of the situation and asked them to investigate his own district. Despite the scorn heaped upon him by local educators, parents, students, community members, and the school board, he continued to support the investigation and pressed for change. The school board's response was to terminate his contract, but eventually, after a great deal of newspaper and television coverage, the practice of tracking was abolished (and, furthermore, Cherubini was reinstated by the board to complete his term). Later he was honored nationally with the John F. Kennedy Profiles in Courage award.

Short of calling in the Justice Department, a change agent can often create conditions for honest and respectful talk by initially detecting and then challenging the power of those with ideological dogma. It can be done through focused work with individuals and groups.

The following is a personal example, written by an assistant principal who happened to be in a meeting with his principal when the incident described occurred. The incident demonstrates how a change agent can acknowledge and challenge the self-importance and power of another and move a discussion from one that is dominated by one individual to one that takes place among equal, interested persons.

Have I ever been surprised by the principal's behavior? You don't know! He is something. I was sitting in his office one morning, not really doing anything, just talking. All at once, this man bursts into the office. Fancy suit, red in the face, obviously angry. It startled the principal and me. He had just brushed by the secretary and charged right in. He never even looked at me. He just stood across the desk from the principal and said, in a real loud voice, almost yelling, "I want to see you! I'm so-and-so's father, and I'm an attorney."

The principal didn't do anything, didn't get up, didn't even move. Then, in a real calm voice, he said, "And I like Mexican food." The man just exploded: "What in the god-damned hell has that got to do with anything?" Then the principal stood up, leaned across the desk, and said, "About as much as you being an attorney. . . . If you want to come in here and tell me you're an attorney, then [wait] while I call our attorney, 'cause I won't spend thirty seconds of my time on you. That intimidation crap isn't going to work here. But if you want to come in here as so-and-so's father to talk to so-and-so's principal so we can work together to solve whatever the problem is, sit down and we'll visit. That's what I'm here for. Now, what do you want to do?"

I thought, oh Christ, this is going to be something. There were a couple of what they call "pregnant seconds," and then you could just see the man deflate. He apologized and sat down and said he'd like to talk with the principal about some problem his son was having with a teacher. The principal looked at me, asked if I would excuse them, and I left. The principal's secretary told me an hour later that they came out of the office, laughing like they were old school chums and everything was just fine. I don't think I'll ever forget that! [Hartzell, Williams, & Nelson, 1995, p. 117].

The principal made it clear that being an attorney did not make this person's opinion about the education of his child any more important than if he had been a baker, taxi driver, or textile employee. The principal refused to succumb to hierarchical status and self-importance. Instead, he acted forcefully to recenter the discussion from power to the issue of a shared obligation between two humans, an educator and a parent, to find out what is best for another, a student.

Likewise, in meetings of school and community members to determine educational programs that would provide more rigorous, active, and challenging learning for all, the role of a facilitator is to keep the discussion shared among concerned equals and not one in which the bank president, the head of the teachers' union, the minister, the principal, or the rocket scientist have greater importance and influence than anyone else at the table, whether they be a paraprofessional, a mother, a veteran teacher, or a student. It's critical to be aware of how such factors as gender, race, ethnicity, and family background also may create unequal distribution of influence and the need for a change agent to forcefully reallocate dominance so that all are truly equal participants. Of course, members of a group will vary in the degree of expertise they bring to an issue, and the change agent should see that expertise is known and used, but this is different from allowing those with higher status, power, or money to dominate a group. Instead, the focus of the group should be on how all members, as equals, can learn from one another about how to educate all students better.

Democracy is both a means and an end. It is a means insofar as equality, liberty, and fraternity are used to make decisions; it is an end when changes achieve greater equality, liberty, and fraternity in the learning experiences of all the students in a classroom, school, or community. When democratic means and ends come together, a school is a most powerful and successful community. Nondemocratic means will not achieve democratic ends, however, as the following illustrates: "He says we're all really talented and he wants to know what we think, but he does most of the talking every time we get together. He says we're empowered, but what we're really empowered to do is what he wants us to do" (Hartzell, Williams, & Nelson, 1995, p. 115).

Contrast that dichotomy between the rhetoric of equality and the practice of domination with the following statements by a principal of a school where participation, democracy, and success are a way of life: "I'm a big boy and as an adult I can understand that I cannot always have my way. Then again . . . I'm disappointed when things don't go [my] way. But those are the moments of frustration. . . . I can deal with those. . . . We've had a tremendous period of soul searching and a lot of examination of ourselves, individually and as a leadership team, and as a school. . . . I don't run the school. We all run it together in the best interest of student learning" (quoted in Glickman, Allen, & Lunsford, 1994b, pp. 211–212).

Democratic means must be employed to achieve democratic aims, or democratic decision making will simply reinforce old patterns of passivity, control, and disengaged routines for students. This is why most research on schools using shared decision making and site-based management have found little changes in teaching and learning practices, and learning results for students have been discouraging (see Elmore, 1996; Guskey & Peterson, 1996; Cohen, 1995; Miller, 1995; Levin, 1994). When democracy is stressed only as a process (or a set of bylaws) for making decisions in site-based councils, without a focus on what are to be the educative purposes of those decisions, then the group typically makes decisions that please the adults, reinforce old habits, perpetuate dominant patterns, and reinforce control and power structures within the school and community. But when democracy is understood as more than the process of how we rule but also as the goal of education—to give greater influence, engagement, participation, and freedom to all students—then a school has the capacity to effect powerful new teaching and learning practices and to change the lives of all students profoundly for the better.

As Schwarz wrote about his school, "If I believe I own something, am a part of a community and have a say, I will treat it and my relationship to it differently than if I am just passing through or renting.

And that changes everything from after-school staff development to dealing with the behavior or achievement of students who are not in my class but who are in MY SCHOOL. . . . The most compelling reason to me for following . . . ideas about democracy is that I can help create a powerful community that gets things done more efficiently than one in which there are only powerful individuals" (personal communication, December 27, 1995). How then can equalization of power be accomplished to achieve the means and ends of democratic education?

The following are four roles for democratic change that I personally have found useful. With all of these roles there is a common value dilemma experienced when acting as a democratic change agent (whether as an external facilitator, member, chair, or formal leader). It is the 1960s cliche "If you're not part of the solution, then you're part of the problem." I often participate in discussions and decisions about educational change in meetings of local public schools, in colleges and universities, and at state and national commissions. When I feel strongly that the direction of a decision is wrong, I struggle with how hard I should try to convince others of the rightness and educational soundness of my views, when I should retreat to a more modest stance that might soften and minimize the harm of the direction, and when I should let others convince me that I might be wrong. At what point should I push the issue, resist, declare war, or take a walk?

If I push too hard and only alienate the opposition and harden their position, am I then really a part of the solution? If I clarify, help others understand my feelings, but then back off, am I then still part of the solution? If I take a walk because I'm opposed to the decision being made, am I now part of the problem? These issues are not simple, and they tend to keep me awake at night.

What helps me resolve them is the moral stance that democracy should be the only absolute in American society, as both a means and an end. Thus, I keep such a criteria in the forefront of my thoughts as I work with a group, school, or community, and I use a repertoire of methods, procedures, and behaviors according to the group, its progress, and my role in adhering to that criteria.

ROLES IN FACILITATING CHANGE

Below I explain several roles I have played and the strategies I used in each: (1) a consultant-facilitator to a group, (2) a regular member of a group, (3) the elected chair of a group, and (4) the formal leader of an organization with formal authority.

As a Consultant-Facilitator

As a facilitator, I need to be clear that my role is to help the group attain a wider vision of education than it currently holds. Thus I can freely ask people to explain, discuss, desist, and adhere to the consensus, or to follow any other decision-making rule the group has agreed to prior to beginning substantive deliberations. Members of the group might not be able to do with one another what I as an external facilitator can do. Usually when a group contains one or more people of authority, status, reputation, or control who are perceived as being higher than others, group members naturally will defer to them. I can diminish this excessive influence by clarifying and gaining the group's agreement to a collaborative process and actively redistributing influence by the extent to which I invite and allow different people to speak. Thus, many years ago, when I worked as an outside facilitator to both a high school and elementary school on a weekly basis, I was seen by the school administrators, faculty, staff, and parents as the gatekeeper and mediator of influence—the buffer between traditional power and emergent (and at first hesitant) participation by others.

The advantage of having external facilitation is that the facilitator, as a nonmember, can hold individuals to the structure, process, and overall aims of deliberation as agreed to by the group in inviting the facilitator. This is why it is so important to have those understandings about the appropriate role of the group facilitator before beginning a long-term relationship with the group. After all, the strength of a facilitator's role is also the potential weakness of the role. If persons of formal power within the group do not accept or comply with the facilitator's directions, they can take over the process and move decisions away from democratic aspirations. The facilitator, without any formal authority, has little recourse in such a situation except to reiterate previous understandings and open such misbehavior to the scrutiny of the group. But again, since the facilitator has no organizational authority, he or she has no ultimate formal authority to prevent persons of power from dominating discussions or the direction of decisions. Without success in reducing domination, the only choice that a facilitator has is to ask for new clarification of roles, and if he finds them unacceptable, resign.

As a Member of a Group

If I'm simply a member of an education group, without formal leadership duties or an assigned role, then I have less control over the process but more freedom to influence the decision. I can press my own point of view, disagree with others, and make suggestions for more research, information, or external help. However, as a member of the group I need to be aware of the necessity of respecting democracy as a process. For example, I need to be careful not to speak at length, to be aware of others who have not spoken much, and to give up "floor time" to less vocal persons. I also need to respect opinions different from my own by listening carefully to those who disagree with my point of view and letting them know that I understand their point of view. At the end, my final criteria in determining whether to approve a group proposal is that it have the elements of either (1) consciously advancing democratic aspirations through changes in our educational programs or (2) at least putting into action a plan to study practices that I believe to be currently not fair and not challenging to all students. If I can't find either elements in the proposed decision, then in good conscience I cannot approve it and need to publicly give my reasons for my opposition. If the process of approval is by group consensus, then by disapproving I effectively veto the decision, and we as a group must go back to figuring out what to do. If the process is not by consensus (for example, majority rule), my disapproval cannot stop a decision from being made, and all I can do is ask the group for reconsideration. If this is not forthcoming, I then need to register a protest with the group and take my disagreement to the next appropriate authority or to other public media and forums. This resistance and appeal is not meant to intimidate, threaten, or coerce others to back down from their decision; it is simply a process for reconsideration, and it is the same for every other member of a democratic group.

As Elected Chair of a Group[1]

The role of an elected chairperson of a group has its own set of dual responsibilities and methods of operations. When I have such a role, I know that my position as chair is to articulate the issues to be decided upon with group members, to bring study and deliberation to those issues, and then to see that decisions, tasks, and policies are made according to a defined process. My other responsibility is to be a group member, free to press my own perspective in the group deliberations. What I have to be most careful about is that these dual roles of chairperson and group member are not used to unfair advantage—such as to limit the airing of ideas I personally dislike or to assume that the group agrees with the ideas I do like. I have to make sure that I do not use the role of chair to bury misunderstandings and avoid resistance from others. This is difficult to do, as I need to watch myself work as both chair and member. A technique that I often use in this dual role is to ask the group at each meeting to process with me the group's operations to see if priorities are clear, if ideas are being freely entertained, and if there are unknown or unforeseen hurdles that need to be worked through. At the end of deliberations and after final decisions are made, the chair has to respect the agreed-upon process for moving a decision along—regardless of his or her personal stance. However, as a group member, if the direction is not satisfactory, then I can ask for appeal and reconsideration, just as any other group member might do. If such is the case, I usually resign the chairmanship so that I can fully exercise my equal rights as a group member.

As Formal Leader of an Organization

The idea of any single person with organizational authority making decisions that affect other people might seem antithetical to the notion of democracy as education. But singular (or jointly held) formal leadership positions in a school are important to a purposeful democratic community when they are used for one purpose only, to implement the vision—as defined by all—of the school. With this purpose in mind, authority is vested by the community in one person or a select few to carry out the administration, implementation, and coordination of overall plans. For example, most teachers, staff, parents, students, and community members are more valuable to a school when they spend their time on overall educational plans and practices of education rather than in countless committees determining mundane issues such as what copy machine to purchase. What I'm speaking of here about formal leadership is a very different type of authority—not hierarchical authority conferred from the top down, by the district, board, union or state, but authority conferred from the bottom up, from the school and community (Sergiovanni, 1996; Lieberman, 1995). Protecting the community's vision means serving only as long as the people wish you to serve; thus evaluations of "bot-

tom-up leaders" should be held at least yearly. If more people disap-
prove than approve of the work of the formal leader in promoting and
enhancing the vision of the school, then the leader should automatically resign.

When a formal leader has divested himself or herself of top-down,
external authority and depends on internal authority, he or she is free
to do what is necessary to carry out democracy as education. This
includes convening groups, raising issues, suggesting ways of organizing for work, and developing with the group a framework and plan
for school improvement (see Glickman, 1993). This also includes having the authority to supervise and coach teachers and staff in their
professional growth as well as to counsel and, if necessary, terminate
the employment of persons (with all regard to fairness and due
process) who are antidemocratic in their relationships and actions
with students and colleagues (Glickman, Gordon, & Ross-Gordon,
1995).

WHEN ALL IS SAID AND DONE

In analyzing facilitation, change, and leadership across various roles
as facilitator, group member, chairperson, and formal leader, the moral
stance of democracy as the absolute good in education is the guiding
light to purposeful action. Each person needs to be aware of his or her
behaviors as well as those of others in striving for democracy—as both
means and ends, as a way of learning and living among people. When
the process of democracy doesn't move toward democratic ends or
reflect equal participation, then confrontation and challenge are
needed. Democracy as education does not happen automatically, by
itself; it needs force, activation, and direction. It's a job for all those
who serve the vision of a people of becoming greater than before.

Note

1. This is a position that I personally have held as a public school principal
   and, more recently, as head of the Program for School Improvement (PSI)
   at the University of Georgia. PSI operates, among other initiatives, the
   League of Professional Schools. The League is a democratically focused
   school renewal network of over one hundred member schools working
   together (at regional meetings, in on-site visits and facilitation, in case

study and action research exchanges, in development of curriculum and assessment standards, and so on) with a financial budget (derived in part by school membership fees) and with a clear, common direction of educational work that each member school commits itself to. Thus to be a "League school" means a voluntary commitment by the school (approved by at least 80 percent of all faculty by secret vote) to do democracy as education schoolwide, by establishing a covenant of beliefs, a charter for shared governance, and a critical study process of action research (Lunsford, 1995). Hopkins, Ainscow, and West have referred to the League as "a sort of school improvement club where the rules of admission define a generalized approach to development work in schools" (1994, p. 76).

—⁓— Conclusion: Democracy as Education

The theologian Harvey Cox points out that contemporary values, without a strong connection to a historic, fundamental vision of life, are faddish opinions with short life spans: "Values are rooted in narrative.... Without roots, disembodied 'values' become mere preferences and eventually dissolve into the ether" (1995, p. 69). Unfortunately, contemporary values about public education are a case in point. Each wave of "new" beliefs, needs, changes, innovations, and refocusing are replaced by the next wave; the result is public schools that are either constantly turning with the wind or keeping to secure routines and "waiting out" the new winds of reform. What has been lost to educators, parents, and citizens in all of this is the connection of education to an original belief about the purpose of schools. David Mathews, citing the Northwest Ordinances of 1787, stated that the purpose of education in the United States of America is to

- Create and perpetuate a nation dedicated to particular principles
- Develop a citizenry capable of self-government
- Ensure social order
- Equalize educational opportunity for all
- Provide information and develop the skills essential to both individual economic enterprise and general prosperity [adapted from Mathews, 1996, p. 12]

The failure of American education has not been in the underachievement of individual students but rather in the failure to acknowledge the purpose of public education in "completing the great work of the American Revolution" (p. 20).

It has been my contention, in this collection of personal observations, that we need to return to the central idea of public education for democracy (Dewey, 1916) and that to accomplish this we must view democracy *as* education, the most powerful form of education. As the education historian Cuban wrote, "When teachers and principals choose a pedagogy rooted in a vision of children as individuals who need to make their own decisions, who need to connect what occurs in classrooms with activities outside the school, and who need to discover and create knowledge rather than absorb it [they] produce very different schools and students from those educators who view children as small people who have to be filled with correct knowledge and trained to be big people" (1989, p. 375).

AN AMERICAN EDUCATION:
THE FUNDAMENTAL HOPE OF A PEOPLE

When professionalism in education is seen as completing democracy, as establishing standards of practice and altering curricula, instructional programs, and teaching and learning methods to further the purpose of democracy, the accumulative results for students are stunning. Schools in inner cities, rural towns, and suburbs—wealthy and poor—show substantial evidence of student achievement (as measured by academic examinations, recognitions and honors, attendance and completion rates, and postgraduation accomplishments) when a pedagogy of democracy is implemented. But such achievements do not occur unless people at the local level take control of their own destiny and work toward the aspiration of purposefully educating their youth to become better citizens in our democracy.

The paradox of educational renewal is that there is not anything particularly new to learn about powerful education. We don't need new innovations or reforms; rather, we need to return to old ideas about people, equality, fraternity, and liberty to create freedom. Using a democratic process to decide upon a pedagogy of democracy for achieving democratic purposes is the only way that all students can be educated well. So why don't more educators, schools, districts, and states do so? I think that it has to do with a lack of understanding about the purpose of public education. "Radical decentralization" to the will of the local school community, according to the democratic view, is not radical at all. It is simply the way that a democracy of the people is supposed to be. The democratic application by students of learning that is active, participatory, and expressive of student choices and contributions is no more experimental than democracy itself.

Democracy is always an experiment. The idea that all children—not some—within classrooms, schools, and states should receive the most interesting, the most challenging, and the most responsible education possible should not be a startling idea. The response should be, "Well, of course—whatever other kind of education could there be in America?"

The resistance of so many teachers, administrators, parents, and others to giving local schools support and incentives for making their own decisions instead of giving them more uniform prescriptions, rules, mandated assessments, and set curricula comes from fear of losing control—fear that local parents, students, and educators can't be trusted, and fear that such autonomy would create chaos. It is the fear that to let the people rule will result in a lack of coordination and eventually to balkanization.

In my experience, I have seen more coordination among curricula, assessment tools, and materials in democratic schools then in nondemocratic ones, and greater articulation of the goals of education. School people (faculty, students, parents) who are clear about their purpose care about the prior preparation and future transitions of their students; they want to ensure that students learn what they need to move on to the next stage of their life or education. Democratic schools coordinate curricula and student progress with feeder and receiving schools in practice much more than schools forced to coordinate by the requirements of districts, unions, or states. I believe the whole issue of centralization for coordinating efforts is actually just a rationale for protecting existing positions and authority and district, union, and state control. After all, the most reputable private schools (the ones so many key educational policymakers send their own children to) are not required to coordinate with anyone. These schools instead develop programs on their own that will help their students succeed at the next level of schooling—whatever and wherever that might be.

PUTTING CALAMITY ASIDE

I don't believe "the sky is falling" on America. In my lifetime, there has not been a period that I can remember when politicians, economists, historians, and sociologists have not claimed that as a country we were in the most serious of peril. I heard this during the era of the Cold War, during the era of depleted resources and solar warming, during the era of the civil rights movement and the anti-Vietnam movement, during the era of double-digit inflation and recession, and during the era of assassinations of national leaders. I heard about the imminent meltdown of society after Watts, Detroit, Rodney King, Waco, and so on. And once again, I hear very familiar-sounding reports about the perils of existing in America, increased fragmentation along racial and class lines, invasions of illegal aliens, domestic poverty and violence, and international wars of devastation. I admit to some skepticism when I hear once again that we as a nation are now in an unprecedented crisis hurtling toward our doom. It seems that such statements come from a perspective that the only way for Americans to change is to claim that this is our last opportunity for doing so before we descend into the eternal inferno. I'm weary of such reports.

We either have a poor understanding of American history, or we wish simply to ignore it (Powers, 1995; Coontz, 1995). Our country is not being torn apart today as it was during the Civil War (when we did kill one another in numbers thankfully never repeated since). Does anyone really think that today's concerns about a slow economy come close to the Depression, the national bankruptcy that was turned around only by emergency legislation and World War II? Do we think that race discrimination is worse now then when segregation was legal and lynching of fellow citizens was ignored? Have we forgotten about the cruel exploitation of children and laborers, the past hatreds against aboriginal people, and the overt oppression of Irish, Italian, Jewish, African, and Asian immigrants? Is it really worse today?[1]

America is in a perilous time, but it has always been in such times. This doesn't mean that we should minimize our problems and accept despicable conditions accorded to humans within and outside our country. But America as a nation has existed for two hundred years, and it most likely will exist two hundred years from now. There is enough strength and responsiveness in the American mix of special interests, capitalism, representative government, and public agitation to maintain the nation. So if you are looking for a doomsday scenario, a description of a great calamity lurking behind the nation's corner unless we wake up immediately and dramatically change our schools, you'll be disappointed.

I'm less concerned with crisis response and more concerned with whether America will be a true democracy, whether we will narrow the gulf between our rhetoric and our day-to-day practices. Our American public schools today, on the whole, are not a disaster; some are, but most are not (Berliner, 1993; Rand, 1994; Jennings, 1996). Most schools make it through each year, and most parents are quite satisfied with the education their local school provides for their children. All kinds of statistics are bandied about, in typical fashion, about the crisis in public schools. In true alarmist tones, schools are portrayed as falling into the abyss as never before; unless we do what the particular doomsayer urges, we are told, terrible calamity will befall us. All of our students will become ignoramuses, we will lose our workforce, and America will be no more (Cuban, 1994). Do Americans really believe this to be true? There is ample data around that indicates that over the past decade, American public schools have been doing fine. They have graduated more students, achievement has been higher, minority students have made gains, and more of our students are doing advanced work and attending higher education than ever before (National Center for Education Statistics, 1995, 1996; "Math Scores on SAT Rise . . . ," 1996; Jennings, 1996).

Furthermore, most parents trust the schools their children attend (Johnson & Immerwahr, 1994, p. 36; Elam, Rose, & Gallup, 1996). I don't think these are signs of a national education crisis. I don't want to minimize the real and terrible situations that do exist. Some schools are in horrible condition, most notably in urban and rural settings, with little resources to cope with danger, stress, and inadequate materials. Many of them do need emergency attention, but these situations are not the norm.

Let me suggest that if not a single school changed in America, public education would not collapse. It didn't collapse during the turn-of-the-century influx of immigration, it didn't collapse during the Sputnik crisis, it didn't collapse during forced integration, it didn't collapse during student walkouts and fire bombs, and it won't collapse today because of violence, the perception of disarray, and advocacy of privatization. *American public education is here to stay; what we do with and for it will be the test of our aspirations for a democratic society.*

THE REAL RENEWAL OF AMERICA'S SCHOOLS

So let's put calamity talk aside and talk about something much more fundamental: What should our schools be? Unless public education changes, we will continue to be a country of restricted access to knowledge and participation. We will continue to live undemocratically behind the rhetoric of democratic ideals. Democracy is practice, not merely belief. It is common citizens living, working, and learning together and ruling themselves in ways more just and equitable than those delivered by oligarchies, monarchies, aristocracies, or dictatorships. A democracy protects free expression, general diffusion of knowledge, the marketplace of ideas, and the open pursuit of truth so that its citizens can continually educate themselves in order to better participate and govern, in ways that go beyond the limited ideas of individuals. We do need to revolutionize our schools in the sense of revolving or returning to the original point. Our fundamental purpose is to reclaim the natural rights of men and women to be free. We don't have an American society that truly practices the ideals of equality, justice, and liberty, and we don't have public schools that promote such beliefs through pedagogy. It is not a matter of whether America will survive, it is a matter of whether democracy will ever become a way of life in America.

—⁓—

Education as democracy—in organization, structure, and pedagogy—must come from the deliberation of local educators, parents, students, and citizens. If we make decisions guided by justice and equality for all in striving for life, liberty, and the pursuit of happiness and if we practice democracy as a pedagogy of learning, it will change our schools, our students, and our society. Will it occur? The choice rests with you and me.

So will the discussions you have read in this book make a major and immediate difference in the daily occurrences and overall quality of education for students throughout the land? Probably not. Those who know me might be surprised by such pessimism. But after nearly thirty years of involvement in sustaining democratic work with public schools, I know the toll such work takes on people, and I know that most schools, districts, boards, and local communities have a hard time discussing or believing in democracy. It is hard to act democratically, particularly when others see democracy as softness, foolishness, or naivety.

There are perhaps more schools involved in these efforts than ever before, but such schools, at most, account for 10 percent of all our public schools. This number will not increase much more, and it may decrease unless local educators, students, and parents are willing to band together within and across schools and have earnest conversations about why public schools exist (Hampel, 1995). To attain the purpose of public schools will mean pushing districts, unions, and state policymakers to consider how democracy delegated to willing schools at the local site level is the only responsible way to educate students. And it means that previous controllers will need to lay control aside and support local schools' change efforts with recognition, flexibility, authority, support, and accountability.

So many teachers, principals, parents, and citizens have articulated to me the power of linking education and democracy. These persons often have been voices in the wilderness of mainstream education thought and practice. Their thoughts and actions have influenced me greatly. My thoughts are not pioneer ones; I do not walk alone. I walk in the tradition of a people's democracy—with all its contradictions, struggles, and possibilities, and with its fundamental belief in the power of an educated citizenry to check evil, the belief that ordinary citizens, when educated, can create an extraordinary society.

Someday I will leave this work, and I'll be glad that my ideas alone did not make the greatest difference. The inventor of the personal essay, Michael de Montaigne, wrote in 1580 that regardless of the topic or subject, "it is myself that I portray" (quoted in McCloskey, 1995, p. 21). These discussions of democracy, learning, wealth, "isms," race, gender, ancestors, change, power, and leadership convey my conception of the past and the possibilities for the future. In a democracy, one person's ideas should never make the greatest difference. Instead, what I hope for is that Americans will become tired—tired of yelling at and retreating from one another; tired of the political left and the right accusing each other of immorality; tired of cultural, racial, and gender groups accusing each other of genocide; and tired of religious and secular groups slinging conspiratorial theories about each other back and forth. I do not want schools to look like my version of democracy. Instead I want educators, parents, and local citizens of all persuasions, politics, groups, and beliefs to participate as equals in helping schools reach and create a generation of citizens that will make us all proud.

Note

1. According to the U.S. Census Bureau and the U.S. Labor Department, the overall health of American society is quite mixed. The unemployment rate

is low, the life expectancy is at an all-time high, and per-person income (adjusted for inflation) has doubled in forty years. On the other hand, crime rates are high (St. George, 1996; Skidmore, 1996). In my own state of Georgia, the educational attainment rates of citizens has increased with gains by minority groups (Williams, 1996). Nationally, there have been great gains in high school graduates' completion of core curriculum and a decrease in the dropout rate. American students now rank among the best in the world in reading, and the gains of minority students have been particularly noteworthy. As U.S. General Counsel for Education John Jennings concluded, "In other words, we are not going to hell in a hand basket" (1996, p. 13).

━ᗵᗵ━ References

Aiken, W. F. (1942). *The story of the eight-year study.* New York: Harper and Brothers.

Allen, L., & Glickman, C. D. (1997). Capturing the power of democracy for school renewal. In A. Hargreaves (Ed.), *International handbook of educational change.* Dordrecht, The Netherlands: Kluwor Academic Publishers.

American Association of University Women. (1992). *How schools short-change girls.* Washington, DC: Author.

American Association of University Women. (1996). *Growing smart: What's working for girls in schools.* Washington, DC: Author.

Arendt, H. (1963). *On revolution.* New York: Penguin Books.

Ayers, W. A. (Ed.). (1995). Popular education: Teaching for social justice [Special issue]. *Democracy and Education, 10*(2).

Banks, J. A. (1994). *Multi-ethnic education: Theory and practice* (3rd ed.). Needham Heights, MA: Allyn & Bacon.

Barber, B. R. (1992). *An aristocracy of everyone: The politics of education and the future of America.* New York: Ballantine.

Barber, B. R. (1993). America skips school. *Harper's, 287*(1722), 39–46.

Bauman, P. C. (1996). *Governing education: Public sector reform or privatization.* Needham Heights, MA: Allyn & Bacon.

Beatty, J. (1995). The road to a third party. *The Atlantic Monthly, 276*(2), 101–104.

Benhabib, S. (1992). *Situating the self: Gender, community, and postmodernism in contemporary ethics.* New York: Routledge.

Berliner, D. C. (1993). Mythology and the American system of education. *Phi Delta Kappan, 74*(8), 632–640.

Bethel School District v. Fraser, 478 U.S. 675 (1986).

Betts, J. (1996, April 7). The South's golden age: A new report confirms the region's incredible renaissance. *The Atlanta Journal-Constitution,* pp. D1–D2.

Board of Education, Island Trees Union Free School District no. 26, et al.
v. *Pico, By His Next Friend Pico, et al.*, 457 U.S. 853 (1982).

Bradsher, K. (1995, April 17). Rich getting richer in United States, studies find. *San Francisco Chronicle*, pp. A1, A6.

Brewer, D. J., Rees, D. I., & Argys, L. M. (1995). Detracking America's schools: The reform without cost? *Phi Delta Kappan, 77*(3), 210–215.

Bruner, J. (1960). *The process of education.* New York: Vintage Books.

Carnegie Forum on Education and the Economy. (1986). *A nation prepared: Teachers for the 21st century.* New York: Author.

Carter, F. (1976). *The education of little tree.* New York: Delacorte Press.

Carter, S. (1993). *The culture of disbelief: How American law and politics trivialize religious devotion.* New York: Basic Books.

Castañeda, J. C. (1995). Ferocious differences. *The Atlantic Monthly, 276*(1), 68–76.

Chase, S. (1996, June 27). Cohen campaigns for children: Business leaders push for defense cuts. *The Burlington Free Press*, p. B1.

Cochran-Smith, M. (1995). Color blindness and basket making are not the answers: Confronting the dilemmas of race, culture, and language diversity in teacher education. American Educational Research Journal, 32(3), 493–522.

Cohen, D. K. (1995). What is the system in systemic reform? *Educational Researcher, 24*(9), 11–17, 31.

Comer, J., and others (Eds.). (1996). *Rallying the whole village: The Comer process for reforming education.* New York: Teachers College Press.

Cook, B. (1996, July 8). Women: Let your voices be heard. *St. Albans Messenger*, p. 4.

Coontz, S. (1995). The American family and the nostalgia trap. *Phi Delta Kappan, 76*(7), K1–K20.

Cornbleth, C., & Waugh, D. (1995). *The great speckled bird: Multi-cultural politics and education policy making.* New York: St. Martin's Press.

Countryman, E. (1996). *Americans: A collision of histories.* New York: Hill & Wang.

Cox, H. (1995). The warring visions of the religious right. *The Atlantic Monthly, 276*(5), 55–69.

Cremin, L. A. (1964). *The transformation of the school: Progressivism in American education 1876–1957.* New York: Vintage Books.

Cuban, L. (1989). The persistence of reform in America's schools. In D. Warren (Ed.), *American teachers: Histories of a profession at work.* Old Tappan, NJ: Macmillan.

Cuban, L. (1993). *How teachers taught constancy and change in American classrooms, 1890–1990* (2nd ed.). New York: Teachers College Press.

Cuban, L. (1994). The great school scam: The economy is turned around but where is the praise? *Education Week, 13*(38), 44.

Cushman, K. (1995). What research suggests about essential school ideas. *Horace, 11*(3), 1–8.

Darling-Hammond, L. (1993). Reframing the school reform agenda: Developing capacity for school transformation. *Phi Delta Kappan, 74*(10), 753–761.

Darling-Hammond, L. (1994). *Professional development schools: Schools for developing a profession.* New York: Teachers College Press.

Darling-Hammond, L. (1996). The right to learn and the advancement of teaching: Research, policy, and practice for democratic education. *Educational Researcher, 25*(6), 5–17.

Darling-Hammond, L. (1997). *The right to learn: A blueprint for reform.* San Francisco: Jossey-Bass.

Dayton, J. (1995). Democracy, public schools, and the politics of education. *Review Journal of Philosophy and Social Science, 20*(1), 135–156.

Dayton, J., & Glickman, C. D. (1994). Curriculum change and implementation: Democratic imperatives. *Peabody Journal of Education, 9*(4), 62–86.

Delpit, L. (1994). *Other people's children: Cultural conflict in the classroom.* New York: New Press.

Derene, K. (1996). Charting a new course: Parents and educators look at charter schools in Wisconsin. *Wingspread Journal, 18*(3), 21–22.

Dershowitz, A. M. (1991, September 20). Political correctness, speech codes, and diversity. *Harvard Law Record,* pp. 405–406.

Dewey, J. (1900). Psychology and social practice. Address of the president before the American Psychological Association, New Haven. *Psychological Review, 7,* 105–124.

Dewey, J. (1916). *Democracy and education: An introduction to the philosophy of education.* Old Tappan, NJ: Macmillan.

Dewey, J. (1968). *The school and society.* Chicago: University of Chicago Press. (Original work published 1900)

Elam, S. M. (Ed.). (1993). *The state of the nation's public schools: A conference report.* Bloomington, IN: Phi Delta Kappa.

Elam, S. M., Rose, L. G., & Gallup, A. N. (1996). The 26th annual Phi Delta Kappan Gallup Poll of the public's attitude toward the public schools. *Phi Delta Kappan, 78*(1), 41–59.

Elmore, R. (1996). Getting to scale with good education practice. *Harvard Educational Review, 66*(1), 1–25.

Elshtain, J. B. (1996, May 5). The politics of resentment is killing democracy. [Adopted from paper presented as a forum at the National Humanities Center, Research Triangle Park, NC.] *The Atlanta Journal-Constitution,* p. C4.

Evans, S. (1989). *Born for liberty: A history of women in America.* New York: Free Press.

Farkas, S., with Johnson, J. (1993). *Divided within, besieged without: The politics of education in four American school districts.* New York: The Public Agenda Foundation.

Fine, M. (1994). *Chartering urban school reform.* New York: Teachers College Press.

Finnan, C., St. John, E. P., McCarthy, J., & Slovacek, S. P. (Eds.). (1995). *Accelerated schools in action.* Thousand Oaks, CA: Corwin Press.

Fried, R. L. (1995). *The passionate teacher.* Boston: Beacon Press.

Fullan, M. (1993). *Change forces: Probing the depths of educational reform.* Bristol, PA: Falmer Press.

Fullan, M., & Stiegelbauer, S. (1991). *The new meaning of educational change* (2nd. ed.). Toronto: Institute for Studies in Education.

Gallagher, J. (1995). Comments on "The reform without cost?" *Phi Delta Kappan, 77*(3), 216–217.

Gardner, H. (1995). Reflections on multiple intelligences: Myths and messages. *Phi Delta Kappan, 77*(3), 200–209.

Gardner, H., Krechevsky, M., Sternberg, R. J., & Okagaki, L. (1994). Intelligence in context: Enhancing students' practical intelligence for school. In K. McGilly (Ed.), *Classroom lessons: Integrating cognitive theory and classroom practice* (pp. 105–127). Cambridge, MA: Bradford Books.

Genasci, L. (1995a, June 10). Black execs face hostility, stereotyping despite positions. *Burlington Free Press,* p. 7A.

Genasci, L. (1995b, June 6). Study: Worker treatment hits bottom line. *Burlington Free Press,* p. 8A.

Glickman, C. D. (1981). *Developmental supervision: Alternative practices for helping teachers improve instruction.* Alexandria, VA: Association for Supervision and Curriculum Development.

Glickman, C. D. (1993). *Renewing America's schools: A guide for school-based action.* San Francisco: Jossey-Bass.

Glickman, C. D., Allen, L. R., & Lunsford, B. F. (1994b). Voices of principals from democratically transformed schools. In J. Murphy and K. S.

Louis (Eds.), *Reshaping the principalship: Insights from transforma-tional reform efforts* (pp. 203–218). Thousand Oaks, CA: Corwin Press.

Glickman, C. D., Gordon, S., & Ross-Gordon, J. (1995). *Supervision of instruction: A developmental approach* (3rd. ed.). Needham Heights, MA: Allyn & Bacon.

Glickman, C. D., Lunsford, B. L., & Szuminski, K. A. (1995). Co-reform as an approach to change in education: The origin of revolution. In M. O'Hair & S. Odell (Eds.), *Educating teachers for leadership and change* (pp. 11–24). Thousand Oaks, CA: Corwin Press.

Glickman, C. D., & Mells, R. (1997). Why is advocacy for diversity in appointing supervisory leaders a moral imperative? In J. Glanz & D. Neville (Eds.), *Educational supervision: Perspectives, issues and con-troversies*. Norwood, MA: Christopher-Gordon.

Goodlad, J. I. (1984). *A place called school: Prospects for the future*. New York: McGraw-Hill.

Goodlad, J. I. (1990). *Teachers for our nation's schools*. San Francisco: Jossey-Bass.

Goodlad, J. I. (1996). Sustaining and extending educational renewal. *Phi Delta Kappan, 78*(3), 228–234.

Goodman, E. (1995, June 2). The good life: An ongoing search. *Burlington Free Press,* p. 10A.

Gray, K. (1996). The baccalaureate game: Is it right for all teens? *Phi Delta Kappan, 77*(8), 528–534.

Greene, M. (1973). *Teacher as stranger*. Belmont, CA: Wadsworth.

Greene, M. (1995). *Releasing the imagination*. San Francisco: Jossey-Bass.

Guralnik, D. B., & Friend, J. H. (Eds.). (1962). Webster's new world dic-tionary, college edition. New York: World Publishing Company.

Guskey, T. R., & Peterson, K. D. (1996). The road to classroom change. *Educational Leadership, 53*(4), 10–14.

Gutmann, A. (1987). *Democratic education*. Princeton, NJ: Princeton Uni-versity Press.

Hacker, A. (1992). *Two nations: Black and white, separate, hostile, unequal*. New York: Ballantine.

Hampel, R. L. (1995, February 8). Breadth versus depth: How do we avoid reform "a mile wide and an inch deep"? *Education Week,* p. 48.

Hartoonian, M., & VanScotter, R. (1996). School-to-work: A model for learning a living. *Phi Delta Kappan,* (77)8, 555–560.

Harmer, C. (1994). *The course you take may be your own: Significance of teachings of Jesus, Socrates, and American Indians for modern educa-tion*. Unpublished master's thesis, Goddard College, Plainfield, VT.

Hartzell, G. N., Williams, R. C., & Nelson, K. T. (1995). *New voices in the field: The work lives of first-year assistant principals.* Thousand Oaks, CA: Corwin Press.

Henry, T. (1995, April 12). Teaching time is highest in the United States. *USA Today,* p. 4D.

Henry, W. A., Jr. (1994). *In defense of elitism.* New York: Doubleday.

Hill, N. (1993). Reclaiming American Indian education. In S. Elam (Ed.), *The State of the nation's public schools.* Bloomington, IN: Phi Delta Kappa Society.

Hilliard, A. G. (1994). What good is this thing called intelligence and why bother to measure it? *Journal of Black Psychology, 20*(4), 430–444.

Hirsch, E. D. (1996). *Moral compass stories for a life's journey.* New York: Simon & Schuster.

Hispanic-owned firms outpace business expansion. (1996, July 11). *Burlington Free Press,* p. 5A.

Holmes Group (1986). Tomorrow's teachers. East Lansing, MI: Holmes Group.

Holmes Group (1995). Tomorrow's schools for education. East Lansing, MI: Holmes Group.

hooks, b. (1995). *Teaching to transgress: Education as the practice of freedom.* New York: Routledge.

Hopkins, D., Ainscow, M., & West, M. (1994). *School improvement in an era of change.* New York: Teachers College Press.

Hunter-Gault, C. (1992). *In my place.* New York: Vintage Books.

Hussar, W. J. (1996). *Projections of education statistics to 2006.* Washington, DC: National Center for Education Statistics, U.S. Department of Education, Office of Educational Research and Improvement.

Irvine, J. J. (1990). *Black students and school failure.* New York: Greenwood Press.

Irvine, J. J., & Foster, M. (Eds). (1996). *Growing up African American in Catholic schools.* New York: Teachers College Press.

Jennings, J. (1996). Travels without Charley. *Phi Delta Kappan, 78*(1), 10–16.

Johnson, J., and Immerwahr, J. (1994). *First things first: What Americans expect from the public schools. A report from Public Agenda.* New York: Public Agenda.

Joyce, B., & Weil, M. (1996). *Models of teaching* (5th ed.). Needham Heights, MA: Allyn & Bacon.

Joyce, B., Wolf, J., and Calhoun, E. (1993). The self-renewing school. Alexandria, VA: Association for Supervision and Curriculum Development.

Kane, M. (1996, January 14). Downsizing: Profit vs. pain. *The Atlanta Journal-Constitution,* pp. C1–C2.

Kincheloe, J. L. (1995). *Toil and trouble: Good work, smart workers, and the integration of academic and vocational education.* New York: Peter Lang.

Kozol, J. (1991). *Savage inequalities: Children in America's schools.* New York: HarperCollins.

Ladson-Billings, G. (1994). *The dream keepers: Successful teachers of African American children.* San Francisco: Jossey-Bass.

Ladson-Billings, G. (1995). Toward a theory of culturally relevant pedagogy. *American Educational Research Journal, 32*(3), 465–491.

Landsberg, M. (1995, October 15). A&P study finds nation's social health has seen steady decline. *Athens Daily News-Banner Herald,* p. 5A.

Lappé, F. M., & Martin, P. (1994). *The quickening of America: Rebuilding our nation, remaking our lives.* San Francisco: Jossey-Bass.

Lasch, C. (1995). *The revolt of the elites and the betrayal of democracy.* New York: Norton.

Lee, V. E., & Smith, J. B. (1994). *High school restructuring and student achievement: A new study finds strong links.* (Issues in restructuring schools, Report No. 7, pp. 1–5, 16.) Madison: Wisconsin Center for Education Research.

Lee, V. E., Smith, J. B., & Croninger, R. O. (1995). *Another look at high school restructuring. Issues in restructuring schools.* (Report No. 9, pp. 1, 7–9). Madison: Wisconsin Center for Education Research.

Leinhardt, G. (1993). On teaching. In R. Glaser (Ed.), *Advances in instructional psychology* (Vol. 4, pp. 1–54).

Lemann, N. (1995a, June 11). Taking affirmative action apart. *The New York Times Magazine,* pp. 36–42, 52–53, 62, 66.

Lemann, N. (1995b). The great sorting. *The Atlantic Monthly, 276*(3), 84–100.

Lemann, N. (1995c). The structure of success in America. *The Atlantic Monthly, 276*(2), 41–60.

Levin, B. (1994). Educational reform and the treatment of students in schools. *The Journal of Educational Thought, 28*(1), 88–101.

Levin, H. M. (1991). *Building school capacity for effective teacher empowerment.* Brunswick, NJ: Consortium for Policy Research.

Lieberman, A. (1995). *The work of restructuring schools: Building from the ground up.* New York: Teachers College Press.

Lindblom, C. E. (1995). Market and democracy—obliquely. The 1995 John Gaus lecture. *P.S.: Political Science & Politics, 28*(4), 684–688.

Lipman, L. (1996, January 18). Voters found fearful, hungary for leadership. *The Atlanta Journal-Constitution,* p. A12.

Lipset, S. M. (1996). *American exceptionalism: A double edge sword.* New York: Norton.

Lofquist, B. H. (1994). Book review: Renewing America's schools. *Democracy and Education, 9*(2), 39–43.

Lugg, C. A., & Dentith, A. M. (1996). Workin' for a livin'. *Educational Researcher, 25*(1), 39, 42.

Lunsford, B. (1995). A league of our own: League of professional schools. *Educational Leadership, 52*(7), 59–62.

Massaro, T. M. (1993). *Constitutional literacy: A core curriculum for a multicultural nation.* Durham, NC: Duke University Press.

Math scores on SAT rise to 24 year high. Verbal results lag. (1996, August 23). *The Wall Street Journal,* p. A4.

Mathews, D. (1996). *Is there a public for public schools?* Dayton, OH: Kettering Foundation.

McCloskey, D. N. (1995). Other things equal: Some news that at least will not bore you. *Eastern Economic Journal, 21*(4), 551–553.

McMannon, T. J. (1995). *Morality, efficiency, and reform: An interpretation of the history of American education.* (Work in progress series.) Seattle, WA: Institute for Educational Inquiry.

McNeil, L. M. (1986). *Contradictions of control: School structure and knowledge.* New York: Routledge.

McPherson, J. A. (1996). Of race and friendship. *Harper's, 297*(1749), 78.

Mead, M., & Wolfenstein, M. (1955). *Childhood in contemporary cultures.* Chicago: University of Chicago Press.

Meier, D. (1995). *The power of their ideas: Lessons for America from a small school in Harlem.* Boston: Beacon Press.

Middleton, S. (1993). *Educating feminists: Life histories and pedagogy.* New York: Teachers College Press.

Miller, E. (1995). Shared decision-making by itself doesn't make for better decisions. *The Harvard Education Letter, 11*(6), 1–4.

Minor, E. (1996, September 8). Park Service honors Carter's roots. *Athens Daily News-Banner Herald,* p. 2A.

National Center for Education Statistics. (1995). *Projections of education statistics to 2005.* (NCES report 95–163.) Washington, DC: U.S. Department of Education, Office of Educational Research and Improvement.

National Center for Education Statistics. (1996). *The condition of education.* Washington, DC: U.S. Department of Education, Office of Educational Research and Improvement.

National Commission on Excellence in Education. (1983). *A nation at risk: The imperative for educational reform.* Washington, DC: U.S. Government Printing Office.

National Commission on Teaching and America's Future. (1996). *What matters most: Teaching for America's future.* Summary report. New York: Author.

Newmann, F. M., Marks, H. M., & Gamoran, A. (1995). *Authentic pedagogy: Standards that boost student performance. Issues in restructuring schools.* (Report No. 8, pp. 1–11.) Madison: Wisconsin Center for Education Research.

Newmann, F. M., & Wehlage, G. G. (1995). *Successful school restructuring: A report to the public and educators by the Center on Organization and Restructuring of Schools.* Madison, WI: Wisconsin Center for Education Research.

Nieto, S., & Rólon, C. (1995, November 11). *The preparation and professional development of teachers: A perspective from two Latinos.* Paper presented to the CULTURES conference "Defining the knowledge base for urban teacher education," Emory University, Decatur, GA.

Noddings, N. (1992). *The challenge to care in schools.* New York: Teachers College Press.

Nord, W. A. (1995). *Religion and American education: Rethinking a national dilemma.* Chapel Hill: University of North Carolina Press.

Oakes, J., & Guiton, G. (1995). Matchmaking: The dynamics of high school tracking decisions. *American Educational Research Journal, 32*(1), 3–33.

O'Brien, C. C. (1996). Thomas Jefferson: Radical and racist. *The Atlantic Monthly, 278*(4), 53–74.

Orfield, G. (1993). *The growth of segregation in American schools: Changing patterns of separation and poverty.* Alexandria, VA: National School Boards Association.

Pang, V. O. (1994). Why do we need this class? Multi-cultural education for teachers. *Phi Delta Kappan, 76*(4), 289–292.

Pang, V. O. (1995, November 11). *Caring for the whole child: Asian Pacific American students.* Paper presented to the CULTURES conference "Defining the knowledge base for urban teacher education," Emory University, Decatur, GA.

Peck, R. S. (1992). *The bill of rights and the politics of interpretation.* St Paul, MN: West.

Peterson, M. D. (Ed.). (1975). *The portable Thomas Jefferson.* New York: Penguin Books.

Peterson, M. D. (1994). Jefferson and religious freedom. *The Atlantic Monthly, 274*(6), 113–124.

Piaget, J. (1974). *To understand is to invent: The future of education.* New York: Viking Press.

Pogrow, S. (1996). Reforming the wannabe reformers: Why education reforms almost always end up making things worse. *Phi Delta Kappan, 77*(10), 656–663.

Postman, N., & Weingartner, C. (1971). *Teaching as a subversive activity.* New York: Penguin Books.

Powers, J. (1995, March 12). Great expectations and how we become so disappointed. *The Boston Globe Magazine,* pp. 18, 31–38.

Putnam, R. D. (1995). Tuning in, tuning out: The strange disappearance of social capital in America. The 1995 Ithiel de Sola Pool Lecture. *P.S.: Political Science and Politics, 28*(4), 664–683.

Quinn, D. (1992). *Ishmael: An adventure of the mind and spirit.* New York: Bantam-Turner.

Rally held for multiracial category on 2000 census. (1996, July 2). *Boston Sunday Globe,* p. A21.

Rand Corporation. (1994). *Student performance and the changing American family: Policy brief of the Institute on Education and Training.* Santa Monica, CA: Institute on Education and Training.

Randall, W. S. (1993). *Thomas Jefferson: A life.* New York: Henry Holt.

Ravitch, D. (1983). *The troubled crusade: American education 1945–1980.* New York: Basic Books.

Ravitch, D., & Thernstrom, A. (Eds.). (1992). *The democracy reader.* New York: HarperCollins.

Raywid, M. A. (1993, September). Finding time for collaboration. *Educational Leadership,* pp. 30–34.

Reno, R. (1995, May 24). IBM's gain came at great loss to many. *Burlington Free Press,* p. 8A.

Rose v. *Council for Better Education,* 790 S.W. 2nd 186 (Ky. Ct. App. 1989).

Rolheiser, C., & Glickman, C. D. (1995). Teaching for democratic life: Effectiveness in context. *The Educational Forum, 59*(2), 196–206.

Rosenthal, H. F. (1996, November 7). *Athens Daily News,* p. 9a.

Rossiter, C. (Ed.). (1961). *The federalist papers: Alexander Hamilton, James Madison, and John Jay.* New York: Mentor Books.

Sarason, S. B. (1990). *The predictable failure of school reform: Can we change course before it's too late?* San Francisco: Jossey-Bass.

Sarason, S. B. (1994). *Psychoanalysis, General Custer and the verdicts of history.* San Francisco: Jossey-Bass.

Sarason, S. B. (1995). *Parental involvement and the political principle.* San Francisco: Jossey-Bass.

Sarason, S. B. (1996). *Revisiting "The culture of the school and the problem of change."* New York: Teachers College Press.

Schlechty, P. (1990). *Schools for the 21st century: Leadership imperative for educational reform.* San Francisco: Jossey-Bass.

Schlechty, P. (1997). *Inventing better schools: An action plan for educational reform.* San Francisco: Jossey-Bass.

Schlesinger, A. M., Jr. (1992). *The disuniting of America: Reflections on a multicultural society.* New York: Norton.

Seeley, D. S. (1985). *Education through partnership.* Washington, DC: American Enterprise Institute for Public Policy Research.

Sennott, C. M. (1996, July 7). The 150 billion dollar "welfare" recipients: U.S. corporations. *Boston Sunday Globe,* pp. 1, 8.

Sergiovanni, T. (1996). *Leadership for the schoolhouse.* San Francisco: Jossey-Bass.

Silko, L. M. (1977). *Ceremony.* New York: Penguin Books.

Sizer, T. (1984). *Horace's compromise: The dilemma of the American high school.* Boston: Houghton Mifflin.

Sizer, T. (1992). *Horace's school: Redesigning the American high school.* Boston: Houghton Mifflin.

Sizer, T. (1996). *Horace's hope.* Boston: Houghton Mifflin.

Skidmore, D. (1996, September 7). Nation's unemployment rate plunges to 7-year low. *Athens Daily News-Banner Herald,* p. 5A.

Slavin, R. E. (1995). Detracking and its detractors: Flawed evidence, flawed values. *Phi Delta Kappan, 77*(3), 220–222.

Slavin, R. E. (1996). *Education for all.* Exton, PA: Swets & Zeitlinger.

Spring, J. (1996). *American education* (7th ed.) New York: McGraw-Hill.

St. George, D. (1996, September 8). Report: Americans seek an anchor amid the seas of change. *The Atlanta Journal-Constitution,* p. B4.

Staff and News Services (1994, June 7). Sara Lee set to trim up to 9,000 positions. *The Atlanta Journal-Constitution,* p. C1.

Stark, S. (1996). Gap politics. *The Atlantic Monthly, 278*(1), 71–80.

Steel, R. (1995). The domestic core of foreign policy. *The Atlantic Monthly, 275*(6), 86–87.

Sternberg, R. J. (1996). Myths, counter myths, and truths about intelligence. *Educational Research, 25*(2), 11–16.

Stevens, R. J., & Slavin, R. E. (1995). The cooperative elementary school: Effects on students' achievements, attitudes, and social relations. *American Educational Research Journal, 32*(2), 321–351.

Study Circles Resource Center. (1995). *Education: How can schools and communities work together to meet the challenge? A guide for involving community members in public dialogue and problem-solving.* Pomet, CT: Study Circles Resource Center.

Survey: More freshmen feeling powerless to change society. (1996, January 5). *Athens Daily News-Banner Herald*, pp. 1, 10.

Swoboda, F. (1994, September 25). Reich takes on competitiveness. *The Boston Sunday Globe*, p. 87.

Szuminski, K. (1993). *The influences perceived by university faculty in establishing a secondary teacher education school-university partnership.* Unpublished doctoral dissertation, University of Georgia.

Timm, J. T. (1996). *Four perspectives on multi-cultural education.* Belmont, CA: Wadsworth.

Torpy, B. (1994, June 8). Sara Lee to shut two Georgia plants. *The Atlanta Journal-Constitution*, p. C1.

Tyack, D. B., & Cuban, L. (1995). *Tinkering toward utopia: A century of public school reform.* Cambridge, MA: Harvard University Press.

U.S. General Accounting Office. (1996, May). *Public education: Issues involving single-gender schools and programs.* (GAO-HHHS-96–122.) Washington, D.C.: U.S. Government Printing Office.

Vygotsky, L. L. (1978). *Mind in society.* Cambridge, MA: Harvard University Press.

Wagoner, J. L., Jr. (1989). *Thomas Jefferson on public education and an enlightened society: Selected quotations.* Unpublished manuscript, University of Virginia.

Walker, T. M. (1996, May 18). Magazine warns of harmful effects as gap between CEO, worker pay grows. *The Atlanta Journal-Constitution*, p. B2.

Wasley, P. (1994). *Teachers who lead: The Rhetoric of Reform and the Realities of Practice.* New York: Teachers College Press.

Wasley, P., Hampel, R., & Clark R. (1997). *Essential connections: Kids and school reform.* San Francisco: Jossey-Bass.

Watson, P., & Barber, B. (1988). *The struggle for democracy.* London, England: Witt Allen.

West, C. (1993). *Race matters.* New York: Vintage Books.

West, C. (1996, March 16). *Race matters in education.* Address to the annual conference of the Association for Supervision and Curriculum Development, New Orleans.

Westbrook, R. B. (1991). *John Dewey and American democracy.* Ithaca, NY: Cornell University Press.

White, B. (1993, December 12). Inner-city schools find harder classes really get results—National school matters. *The Atlanta Journal-Constitution*, p. G4.

White, B. (1996, May 26). Following his own convictions: Profiles in courage. *The Atlanta Journal-Constitution,* pp. G1–G2.

Wigginton, E. (1985). *Sometimes a shining moment.* New York: Anchor Books.

Williams, D. (1996, September 7). Mediocre Georgia graduation rates show improvement. *Athens Daily News-Banner Herald,* p. 5A.

Wills, G. (1979). *Inventing America: Jefferson's Declaration of Independence.* New York: Vintage Books.

Wilson, D. L. (1992). Thomas Jefferson and the character issue. *The Atlantic Monthly, 270*(5), 57–74.

Wisniewski, L. (1993, September 30). Schools receive another failing grade: National goals not being met. *The Atlanta Journal-Constitution,* pp. A1, A13.

Wolfenstein, M. (Ed.). (1955). *Childhood in contemporary cultures.* Chicago: University of Chicago Press.

Wolk, R. A., & Rodman, B. H. (Eds.). (1994). *Classroom crusaders: Twelve teachers who are trying to change the system.* San Francisco: Jossey-Bass.

Wood, G. (1992). Restructuring time, size, and governance: Steps toward democratic schooling. *Democracy and Education, 6*(3), 3–13.

Wood, G. (1993). *Schools that work.* New York: NAL/Dutton.

Woolf, V. (1978). *A room of one's own.* London, England: Granada.

World's women still have far to go. (1995, August 27). *The Atlanta Journal-Constitution,* p. A5.

Zborowski, M. (1949). The place of book-learning in traditional Jewish culture. *Harvard Educational Review, 19*(2), 87–109.

Zinn, H. A. (1980). *People's history of the United States.* New York: Harper-Collins.

Index